OLDEST TAMPA BAY

JOSHUA GINSBERG

Reedy Press
PO Box 5131
St. Louis, MO 63139
www.reedypress.com

Library of Congress Control Number: 2022937095

ISBN: 9781681063638

Cover design: Jill Halpin
Book design: Linda Eckels

Printed in the United States of America
22 23 24 25 26   5 4 3 2 1

Table of Contents

PINELLAS COUNTY

MANATEE AND SARASOTA COUNTIES

Research and Acknowledgments

Telling one linear narrative of a place presents challenges to even the most experienced historians. The Tampa Bay area is not that sort of a place and, frankly, I am not that sort of historian—this work constitutes my first such attempt at a primarily historical work. What I have discovered along the way is an area composed of adjacent counties, cities, and neighborhoods that often differ dramatically in their origin stories.

My task was made more complex by several factors, not the least of which has been the COVID-19 global pandemic, which only accelerated the already head-spinning pace of change here in the Tampa Bay area. Consequently, I've had to revise "the oldest" of several categories multiple times as many local businesses and restaurants closed their doors for good. It is almost a certainty that even before you read this book, some of the chapters will be outdated—such is the difficulty of hitting a moving target like this one.

My research has centered on Hillsborough, Pinellas, Manatee, and Sarasota counties, though earlier drafts covered an even wider area. I've also generally considered "the oldest" to mean "the oldest currently or continually operating in the manner for which it was originally designed." In some cases, to capture people, places, and things I deemed significant to the area's history, I have also included the "oldest preserved" (i.e. The McMullen-Coachman Log Cabin, the prehistoric canoe at Weedon Island, Gamble Mansion, and others). In terms of buildings or other structures that have moved from one location to another (sometimes more than once, like Tampa's oldest single-family home and the Bellevue Inn), I've tackled this on a case-by-case basis. For this same reason I've tried to distinguish between organizations, clubs, and congregations, which often move from one location to another, versus their buildings, which tend to move less frequently.

What ultimately emerges, I hope, is the story of a place that stretches back not hundreds, but rather thousands of years. It is a story that I could not have told without the help of a vast multitude of fellow writers, local business owners, historians, museum docents, and curators. I would also like to thank the patient and supportive team at Reedy Press (Barbara, Josh, Joe, Mischele, Chelsea, and everyone), as well as my own "support staff" composed of my wife, Jennifer, our shih tzu Tinker Bell, and all of my friends and family for whom I am grateful without measure. A longer and more complete list of all those who deserve thanks and credit can be found on my blog at https://terraincognitaamericanus.blogspot.com/.

This book is for all of them, and for all those who seek to see the world around them not only as it is now, but as it was before, and as it may yet be in the future.

INTRODUCTION

I've come to think of exploring a place like finding a rough gemstone. Through research, that gem gets cut and polished. Assuming I've done my job adequately, it's given a number, placed on the store shelf, and eventually makes its way into the hands of a discerning buyer. I hope that you are that buyer, and when you lift my literary lapidary work up to the light, you discover something new through each facet, because that's how writing these books has been for me. Each book reveals to me a new perspective on the place I now call home.

Secret Tampa Bay sharpened my ability to perceive what is hidden, sometimes in plain sight. Tampa Bay Scavenger allowed me to view the area as a gameboard or the setting for some RPG campaign—as something playable. Oldest Tampa Bay has given me yet another perspective—that of a time traveler.

As I worked on this book, it was a fairly common occurrence for me to stop at a corner somewhere and let my mind's eye try to replay all that had transpired at that spot. I could imagine the earliest mound-building people who set up their camp, only to have it grow into a village with permanent homes, farms, and temples. After that, the Spanish and other Europeans arrived, eventually giving way to the American settlers who drove the indigenous people from their ancestral lands as they built military forts, towns, and communities. Wars and skirmishes took place. Roads, bridges, and eventually cities were built. But the film reel in my head keeps going through cycle after cycle of development, overdevelopment, decline, abandonment, and renewal.

My imagining would continue even further, but usually at this point my wife would tap me on the shoulder to ask why I'd been staring at a parking garage for 15 minutes. I'm lucky to have a time traveling partner like that—someone who knows instinctively when to feed me more line and when to reel me back in to the present.

I've found that this temporal journey has made me acutely aware of how brief any single moment or lifetime is in the long course of a place's story. Change is constant and accelerating faster than ever, especially since the COVID-19 pandemic. In just the several years Jen and I have lived here, we've witnessed countless old businesses, buildings, and vintage roadside attractions vanish to make way for new hotels, roads, and commercial buildings. Coney Island Diner in St. Pete—closed. Airstream Ranch—demolished. Haslam's Bookstore—shuttered for over a year now, its future uncertain.

I hope that you will not only be able to read about the places I've compiled here, but also to visit them in person while you can. Once they are gone, some vital part of our own story departs with them, leaving only faded photos and a foggy amnesiac feeling that something important once happened or stood here.

On a brighter note, I also sincerely hope that you will find the Tampa Bay area as fascinating to view through this latest lens as I have, and that it will not only deepen your appreciation and understanding of where we've been, but also of where we're heading next.

That's all I wanted to say before we get started; the rest are just some nerdy, pop-culture, time-traveling references. So please keep your hands and feet inside the DeLorean at all times, no altering the timeline, and under absolutely no circumstances are you to feed the Morlocks. Let's get to it.

HILLSBOROUGH COUNTY

1757

Oldest Map of the Tampa Bay Area

The Maria Celi Map

The earliest known map showing Florida is believed to be the "Martyr Map," published in 1511 by Italian historian and cartographer Peter Martyr d'Anghiera. The map was included as part of his *Legatio Babylonica*, and is notable for a number of reasons. Not only is it the first map of Bermuda and the Caribbean Islands and the first to use the name "Cuba," it also further debunks Ponce DeLeon's claim of discovering "Florida," as this map was available two years prior to his voyage in 1513. Today only 20 copies of the Martyr Map are known to exist, one of which is in the Touchton Map Library inside of the Tampa Bay History Center.

Following the Martyr Map, the Tampa Bay area would still have to wait another two and a half centuries before becoming the subject of a cartographer's pen. Prior to receiving its place on a map, the area did receive its name. "Tanpa" appears to have been first mentioned in writing by Hernando de Escalante Fontaneda who was shipwrecked, captured by the Calusa tribe, and eventually rescued by Florida's first Spanish Governor, Pedro Menéndez de Avilés, around 1566. Escalante described "Tanpa" as being an important town to the North of the Calusa's territory. After the publication of Escalante's memoirs in 1575, today's

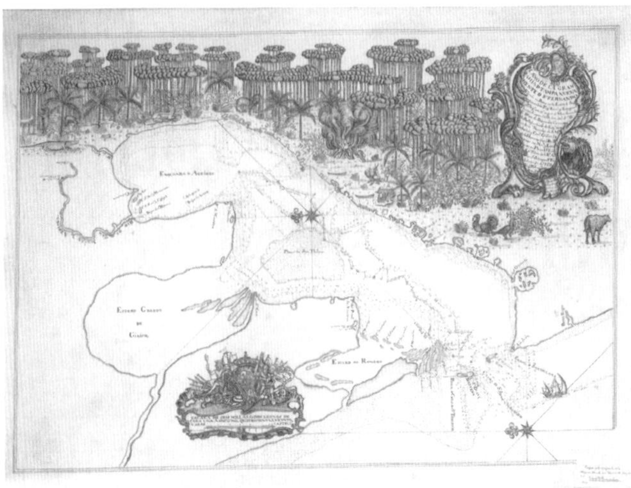

The Celi map includes detailed illustrations of the people and animals encountered on the expedition. File:1757 Celi.jpg, Wikimedia Commons.

Tampa Bay was referred to as both "Bahia Tampa" and "Bahia de Espiritu Santo."

So there was a map of Florida, there was an area known as "Tampa Bay," and at last there was a map of the Tampa Bay area thanks to Don Francisco Maria Celi of the Spanish Royal Fleet. His expedition to the area in 1757 included erecting a cross at what today is Riverhills Park in Temple Terrace. From there he went up the Hillsborough River as far as the rapids in what now is Hillsborough River State Park. His original map is preserved at the Museo Naval de Madrid, but a copy is held by the South Florida History Museum.

The Touchton Map Library is the only cartographic center in the Southeastern United States and an extraordinary historical resource, well worth exploring in person or online.

1842

Oldest Single-Story Family Home

Stringer House

118 S. Westland Ave., Tampa

Old houses accumulate stories. With enough time and enough stories, some are bound to get confused and conflict with one another. Add to this the complexity of untangling the Stringer family history (both a father and son with the name of Dr. Sheldon Stringer) as well as the structure itself having been relocated twice, and there you have the oldest single-family home in Tampa.

According to an article in the *Tampa Tribune* from June 6, 1948, the home was built by the father of Dr. Sheldon Stringer Senior in 1842 on Jackson Street. An earlier article references Dr. Stringer as having lost his father at the age of 11, so by about 1847 we can assume that Dr. Stringer had become the man of the house, just in time to experience the Great Gale of 1848, which was a rare and devastating instance of a hurricane making landfall in Tampa.

The bungalow house seems to have miraculously survived the event, because in 1914 feed store owner Imboden Stalnaker purchased it. Stalnaker dismantled the home, shipped it by train to 3210 E. Eighth Avenue, and reassembled it there. Over time the 2,000 square foot structure became a low-income boarding home and was showing significant damage by 2013 when Darryl Bethune acquired it for $17,000 with plans to restore it. Health

Even behind a chain-link fence at the corner of North Westland Avenue and West Cleveland Street, the Stringer home is a formidable historic structure. Photo by the author.

issues, however, altered those plans and he sold the property to EquiAlt for $55,000.

EquiAlt ran into problems of its own when the federal government came looking to recover money on behalf of hundreds of elderly investors contending that they were victims of a Ponzi scheme led by the company. Rather than spend the estimated $400,000 necessary to restore the home, EquiAlt decided instead to disassemble, relocate, and reconstruct the home (for the second time) at its current location.

Today the structure sits quietly behind a chain-link fence, awaiting a new owner to pen the next chapter in its long story. If owning a piece of Tampa history sounds appealing, as of this writing the home is listed for sale on Zillow for $549,900.

This particular Stringer residence is not the same as the May-Stringer House in Brooksville, which has been turned into a museum.

1843

Oldest Shipyard

Jean Street Shipyard

337 W. Jean St., Tampa

As Tampa gradually took shape around Fort Brooke, its transportation needs grew—both on land and sea. To meet that need, Jean Street Shipyard was established in 1843 (two years before Florida achieved statehood), primarily servicing riverboats and large wooden vessels, which had few ports at the time between Cedar Key and Key West.

The shipyard was ideally situated, sitting on solid ground as far upriver as was navigable and surrounded by bald cypress, longleaf pine, and live oak which provided ample shipbuilding material. One of the shipyard's early owners included Scottish immigrant and schooner captain James McKay, who maintained cargo and trading vessels there. He was elected Tampa's sixth mayor in 1859 and in 1863, his blockade running ships (the *Scottish Chief* and the *Kate Dale*) were torched by union raiders, touching off the only civil war skirmish at Tampa Bay.

By the 1880s shipping returned to and then eclipsed pre-Civil War levels in Tampa. The arrival of the railroads enabled the shipping of phosphate, citrus, and other goods. Busier ports translated to more business for Jean Street Shipyard as well.

Channels dredged in 1904 transformed Tampa Bay into a significant port and accelerated the city's growth. In 1909 the channel up the Hillsborough River to the shipyard was deepened on and the shipyard found a new owner in Harry C. White, a

Photo of Jean Street Shipyard from the Hillsborough River by Capt. J.W. King licensed under CC BY-SA 4.0

skilled boatwright (thought he listed himself as a repairman). By 1928 the shipyard had replaced the "Jean Street" in its signage with "White's." The name changed again following World War II when it became "Johnson's Boat Works," with expanded capabilities to serve the booming motor-yacht market. Among those who serviced boats there was a high-schooler named Charley Morgan who later went on to open his out boat-building business, Morgan Yachts.

In the 1990s, the Seminole Heights neighborhood underwent revitalization and the shipyard along with it. During this time, the shipyard returned to its original name as Jean Street Shipyard.

Just north of the shipyard on the other side of the Hillsborough River is ZooTampa at Lowry Park, which was recently featured in the show Secrets of the Zoo.

1848

Oldest Lighthouse

Egmont Key Lighthouse

Egmont Key State Park, St. Petersburg, FL 33711

Standing 87 feet tall, the lighthouse on Egmont Key has the dual distinction of being both the area's oldest lighthouse and the oldest structure still in use for its original purpose. When it was first erected on a small, uninhabited island at the mouth of Tampa Bay with $10,000 granted by Congress, it was the only one along Florida's Gulf Coast casting a beam of light over the water between St. Marks at the bend of the Panhandle and the Florida Keys.

That the lighthouse would endure for more than 160 years and serve as a beacon to thousands of ships during that time must have seemed a fantasy to Sherrod Edwards, the first lighthouse keeper, as he rowed back to Tampa with his family after surveying the damage caused by a hurricane in September 1848. A second hurricane just four years later caused further damage, threating to topple the tower. Five years later, in 1856,

The Egmont Key Lighthouse continues to serve its function more than 170 years after it was first built. Photo from the US Coast Guard Historic Light Station Information & Photography, public domain.

work to repair the tower began and the structure was moved 90 feet inland to better protect it from beach erosion and storms. Its height was also more than doubled at this time, and starting in 1958, it began using a fixed light from a Fresnel lens.

That lens would be one of many items that lighthouse keeper George V. Rickard would remove from the island in 1861 when, caught between Union-loyal Key West to the South and Confederate St. Marks to the north, he fled the island, which came under Union control.

The island and lighthouse would become part of a comprehensive coastal defense network during the Spanish-American War, during which time Fort Dade was built on the island. The fort was staffed through the First World War but deactivated in 1923. The island became a National Wildlife Refuge in 1974 and was added to the National Register of Historic Places four years later. By the time an automated beacon was installed in 1989, the lighthouse was the last remaining staffed lighthouse in the state and one of only seven in the country.

People sometimes wonder about what looks like an abandoned lighthouse along Hillsborough River just north of downtown, but it never guided any ships—it's the Sulphur Springs Water Tower.

1850

Oldest Public Cemetery

Oaklawn Cemetery

606 E. Harrison St., Tampa

As of the city's first official census count in 1850, Tampa had 974 residents—enough to need a public burial ground beyond the small cemetery at Fort Brooke, which had been created during the Second Seminole War.

Established to serve "White and Slave, Rich and Poor," there is some debate as to which of these categories the first person buried there belonged to. By some accounts, it was a slave who lived on Reverend L.G. Lesley's Alafia River plantation. Other sources point to Nancy C. Hagler, who died giving birth at the age of 16.

In 1874 the St. Louis section of the cemetery was added for Catholic burials. This section includes a monument to five Catholic pioneer priests, which represents the oldest known priests' graves on Florida's west coast. This section is also the resting place of C. Cecilia Morse, who founded the St. Anthony of Padua Catholic School in San Antonio, Florida.

Today, the roughly 1,700 graves contain a great many of those who played vital roles in the development of the area, including Judge Joseph B. Lancaster, the first mayor of Tampa; James McKay Senior, Tampa's sixth mayor; Florida's 16th state governor, Henry Laurens Mitchell; cigar magnate Vicente Martinez Ybor; and local underworld kingpin Charlie Wall.

Pirates, politicians, and pioneers are among those who share common ground at Oaklawn Cemetery. Photo by the author.

It also contains a mass grave and monument for the victims of yellow fever, a section for early pioneer priests, veterans of seven different wars, 102 unknown soldiers from the former Fort Brooke Cemetery, and the reinterred remains of Native Americans which were uncovered during construction of the Tampa Bay Convention Center in 1987.

Other unique markers and memorials include those of pirates, like the Cuban Mr. Hubbard, who was "found dead in woods," [sic] the grave of William and Nancy Ashley, which makes plain the love between master and servant (forbidden in their lifetime), and the grave of Darwin Branch Givens, who "as a young child alerted Tampa of the invading Yankee soldiers with the cry 'the devils are coming.'"

A lesser-known fact about Oaklawn Cemetery is that during a Civil War naval bombardment in 1862, an 8-inch shell landed there among the graves.

1850

Oldest Masonic Lodge

Hillsborough Lodge #25

508 E. Kennedy Blvd., Tampa

The same year that Oaklawn Cemetery was established, the charter for Hillsborough Lodge No. 25 was instituted, making it the oldest Masonic Lodge not only in Tampa but also along Florida's gulf coast. By the end of its first year in existence, its roster had grown to include 61 brothers. The following year a two-story building was constructed at the corner of Whiting and Franklin Streets, and shortly thereafter the original building was replaced with a three-story version.

In 1912 the lodge moved to its third building at its current location on the corner of East Kennedy Boulevard and Morgan Street. That wooden building was replaced with the fourth and current structure, which was erected in 1927 (the cornerstone was laid on June 18, 1928). It was designed by the prolific local architect M. Leo Eliot, who was also a Brother

Close-up view of the Hillsborough Lodge at 508 East Kennedy Boulevard in Tampa, Florida. Photo courtesy of the Tampa-Hillsborough County Public Library System.

there. For inspiration, Elliot looked to three different medieval Italian cathedrals in creating the Mediterranean Revival-style brick building with glazed ornamentation on the walls and ceiling. The lodge's Temple room, unique among Florida lodges, is notable for having been modeled after the Temple of King Solomon with 40 foot-high, hand-painted ceilings and seating for as many as 450 individuals. In September of 1986 the building was added to the US National Register of Historic Places.

The lodge's membership rolls have included many prominent local names over the years. That includes judges, county sheriffs, senators, and multiple mayors (Darwin Branch, E. A. Clarke, Duff Post, Herman Glogowski, and Madison Post) as well as business owner Abe Maas (of the Maas Brothers department stores) and Hillsborough High School Principal Vivian Gaither (for whom Gaither High School is named).

In addition to the Masons, the Tampa Bay Area has been home to other fraternal organizations like the Independent Order of Oddfellows and the Benevolent and Protective Order of Elks.

1865

Oldest African American Baptist Congregation

Beulah Baptist Church

1006 W. Cypress St., Tampa

The Tampa Bay area is home to multiple historic Black churches and congregations, including St. Paul AME Church in Tampa, founded in 1870, and St. Petersburg's Historic Bethel AME Church.

The Beulah Baptist Church became the first Black Baptist Church in Tampa. The Church was organized in 1865, on the heels of the Emancipation Proclamation. Prior to 1865, the all-Black congregation worshipped in the balcony of the First Baptist Church of Tampa. After the slaves were freed, the all-white congregation of the First Baptist Church provided funds for the construction of Beulah's first edifice on Central Avenue. The land was donated by Mrs. Fortune Ranson.

Elder Hadley was called as the first pastor to serve the congregation. Reverend Anderson followed Hadley from 1869 until 1875 and brought new members into the congregation. The church was remodeled the following decade and its frame was moved to a new location in 1881. In 1908, the church was incorporated as a non-profit organization and became Beulah Baptist Institutional Church.

This 1935 photograph from the Burgert Brothers collection shows construction of the Beulah Baptist Church at a previous location on 604 East Tyler Street. Photo courtesy of the Tampa-Hillsborough County Public Library System.

Over the next several decades, the church continued to expand. In 1956 Reverend Dr. A. Leon Lowry Sr. became the church's 13th pastor and held that position for 40 years. As one of Reverend Dr. Martin Luther King Jr.'s theology professors and state president of the NAACP, Lowry was a force for civil rights within and beyond Tampa. Under his leadership a great many auxiliary programs and improvements were implemented and the Burn's Memorial Chapel along with four and a half adjoining lots at Cypress and Delaware were acquired as the site of the new church. In 1990 the A. Leon Lowry Sr. Family Service Center was completed.

Reverend W. James Favorite became the church's next leader in 1996 and presented a "Vision Toward the Year 2000" with a focus on ministry, education, and evangelism. As the Chairman of the Black Leadership Commission on AIDS of Tampa Bay he played a key role in helping reduce the stigma associated with HIV and AIDS. In 2022, Pastor Alan Harris became the church's lead servant. His vision is synonymous with Psalm 127:1: "We Build Here. We are a Movement not a Monument."

Mrs. Fortune Ranson (a.k.a. Madame Fortune Taylor) was a former slave who become a successful business owner and civic leader. She negotiated with Hugh Macfarlane to connect her land downtown to West Tampa via the Madame Fortune Taylor Bridge.

1882

Oldest Public High School

Hillsborough High School

5000 N. Central Ave., Tampa

As one of the oldest high schools in the southern United States, Hillsborough High School has a long and storied history. When principal Mary Cuscaden welcomed the first students in 1882, the institution's official name was "The Hillsborough County High School." It remained so until 1927, when H. B. Plant High School opened. It has also been referred to as "Harvard on the Hill," as it was situated at the highest elevation point in Tampa at the time, shares Harvard's red and black colors (representing the heart and soul), and modeled some of its own traditions after the prestigious university. By the early 1970s it acquired a new nickname, "Peyton Place," based on the opening scene of the eponymous television show, which featured a tower similar to the school's own red brick clocktower.

The first class (of four students) graduated in 1886 under the school's third principal, B.C. Graham. In 1889, it put out the first issue of *The Red & Black*—the first high school newspaper statewide—and in 1907 it had its first football team (which would win its first state championship three years later).

By 1911 the school had outgrown its original space and moved to a building at 2708 Highland Avenue designed by Wilson Potter. This second building is now the home of D. W. Waters

Hillsborough High School's gothic revival style sets it apart from the bungalow architecture found throughout the Seminole Heights neighborhood. Photos by the author.

Career Center, but known locally as "Old Hillsborough County High School." At this second location, the school produced the first yearbook in Florida—the *Hilsborean* (with one "L").

In 1928 the school changed its address for the third and final time to the gothic-style building designed by Francis J. Kennard at 5000 Central Avenue.

The school's alumni constitute a veritable who's who of Tampa, including mayors (Dick Greco, Julian Lane, and William F. Poe), senators, congressmen, judges, business owners, and numerous professional athletes. Other notable graduates include concert violinist and Columbia Restaurant Group Chairman Cesar Gonzmart, actor Rondo Hatton, country singer Slim Whitman, and Medal of Honor recipient 1st. Lt. Baldomero Lopez USMC.

Until 2003, it was commonly held that the school was established in 1885, but documents found inside its cornerstone point to 1882 as the year it began.

1884

Oldest Law Firm

Macfarlane, Ferguson & McMullen

201 N. Franklin St., Tampa

The names that make up Tampa's oldest law firm are likely already familiar to readers, as they are connected to historic homes, parks, business, philanthropic ventures, and major roads. With this in mind, it is perhaps more inevitable than surprising that they should intersect.

Hugh C. "Colonel" Macfarlane was born in 1851 in Scotland and immigrated with his family to the United States. He earned his law degree from Boston University and moved to Tampa in 1884 where he launched his own firm and raised a family. Macfarlane served as city attorney of Tampa for three years and was appointed state's attorney of the Sixth Judicial District in 1893. He also served as a member of the Board of Public works for Tampa and a member of the Board of Port Commissioners, but he is likely best known for founding West Tampa, where

This 1953 Burgert Brothers photograph shows lawyers of law firm Macfarlane, Ferguson, Allison, and Kelly, at Las Novedades Restaurant, 1430 7th Avenue. Photo courtesy of the Tampa-Hillsborough County Public Library System.

he enticed cigar manufacturers to the area and helped build the Fortune Street Bridge, which was the first to cross the Hillsborough River.

Chester Howell Ferguson was born in Georgia in 1908 and joined the firm after receiving his law degree from the University of Florida in 1930. In 1939, he married Louise Lykes, of the Lykes Brothers, Inc. family, one of the area's most prominent agribusinesses. Ferguson handled legal matters for the business and eventually became CEO and chairman of the Board. He also served as CEO and chairman of First Florida Banks Inc., and was a driving force behind the State University System Board of Regents on which he served for 14 years.

The McMullen name was added to the firm when it merged with that of J. Tweed McMullen in 1993. McMullen, a descendent of one of the area's earliest pioneer families, graduated the University of Florida School of Law in 1936, and practiced in Clearwater before he was admitted to practice before the US Supreme Court in 1940. He also served as assistant US attorney for the Southern District of Florida before joining the Navy to fight in World War II, after which he returned to private practice.

With approximately three dozen attorneys in Tampa and Clearwater, the firm's primary practice areas include personal, transactional, and litigation matter.

1889

Oldest Elementary School

Gorrie Elementary School

705 De Leon St., Tampa

From 1880 to 1900 Tampa's population increased dramatically from 800 residents to over 15,000, due in part to the arrival of railroads. With the transition from town to city, residents fanned out from downtown and began raising families in newer suburban neighborhoods such as West Tampa, Tampa Heights, and Hyde Park. Naturally, this created a need for elementary education—a need met by Hyde Park Grammar School.

Research shows that the school may have actually been in operation prior to this, as a Hyde Park Grammar School is referenced as early as 1884 in Board of Public Instruction records. The school quickly outgrew its initial location at the corner of West Seventh (Magnolia) Avenue and Platt Street, which led to the construction of a new building in 1889 at 705 W. De Leon Street, despite protests of parents who felt that this was too far out into the wilderness. While parents may have been upset over the change, the students and educators were no doubt relieved to be attending the first school in Hillsborough County with indoor toilets. The two-story red brick schoolhouse included eight classrooms, to which another eight were added in 1903. Yet another eight classrooms and a cafeteria were added in 1912, and the final portion of the building was completed in 1926.

Gorrie Elementary as it appeared circa 1930. Photo courtesy of the State Archives of Florida, Florida Memory.

In 1915 the school changed its name to Dr. John B. Gorrie Elementary School in honor of his innovative work in medical science, which resulted in the first ice-making machine and paved the way for modern refrigeration and air conditioning.

The building was renovated in 1977, its street car shed was converted into a bus shelter, and in 1989 the roof and exterior walls were repaired. A new Media Center was built in 2002 along with four additional kindergarten classrooms.

Today 561 students attend the school's prekindergarten through fifth grade. It has earned recognitions including the Golden School Award, the Five Star School Award, and the Florida School Recognition Award for sustained and improved academic performance. It is the oldest operating elementary school in the state of Florida.

The elementary school is not the only place to honor Gorrie—he also has a plaque in the Florida Inventors Hall of Fame within the University of South Florida Research Park.

1890

Oldest Phosphate Mining Operation

Mosaic, Inc. (formerly IMC Global Inc., Agrico, Cargill Crop Nutrition, and others)

Bone Valley

Newer area residents are often surprised to learn not only that there are active mines nearby, but of the impact they've had on Florida's economy. At one point, as much as 75% of all phosphate used in the country (for everything from fertilizer to animal feed to toothpaste) came from Florida's "Bone Valley," which spans parts of Hillsborough, Manatee, Polk, and Hardee counties.

Captain J. Francis LeBaron of the US Army Corps of Engineers is regarded as the first to discover phosphate in pebble form while exploring the Peace River in 1881. When additional deposits were identified in 1886 by John C. Jones and Captain W.R. McKee, they formed a business to capitalize on their find. River pebble mining was a complex and costly endeavor, so prospectors began exploring elsewhere. Near present-day Bartow, they found a layer of pebble phosphate just six feet below the surface under sand and clay. The area around Mulberry was found to be the richest, which triggered a rush as fortune-seekers and mining startups descended on the town.

Mostly though, the only thing this first wave of small players ever dug was a financial hole for themselves. Over the next

Shown here are phosphate mining using hydraulics (left) and the dryers and elevator at Pierce as of April 7, 1937 (right). Today Pierce is a ghost town in Polk county. Photos courtesy of Richard Fifer.

decade, larger outfits swooped in, including the major agriculture businesses like Virginia Carolina and American Agricultural Chemical Co, as well as meat packing giants Armor and Swift seeking to augment their bone fertilizer lines. The number of companies operating in Bone Valley dwindled further due to mergers, acquisitions, and depletion of the mines.

Today, Mosaic is the lone company mining Bone Valley, with four active mines. As a renewable resource, there will come a day when the last of the area's usable phosphate has been extracted, refined, and shipped out. Some, concerned over environmental, health, and safety issues, will be glad to see it go. Others view with trepidation how it may impact local jobs and economies. It is, like the quality mines produce over time, a complicated and mixed bag. Regardless of one's opinion on the matter, everyone can agree that mining has shaped the area's past, present, and future.

Although Mosaic was established in 2004, its roots trace back to the area's very first mines. The Mulberry Phosphate Museum is a good place to learn more on the subject.

1891

Oldest Elevator

Henry B. Plant Museum

401 W. Kennedy Blvd., Tampa

When Henry B. Plant opened his Tampa Bay Hotel, it was intended to be the crown jewel in his railroad and hotel empire. As such, it was outfitted with an array of marvels, both natural and technological. That later category included electrical light in each of the 511 rooms and suites, telephones, so-called "fireproof" construction, and an elevator, which was a rare and innovative feature at the time.

Though the hotel itself no longer operates (it is now home to the Henry B. Plant Museum and the University of the Tampa) the elevator has carried on more or less uninterrupted, which makes it the oldest along Florida's west coast and places it among the

The elevator's opulent interior appears as ready to welcome guests today as it was in 1891. Photo by the author.

oldest operating passenger elevators in the country. There was a second freight elevator, which was removed when the state-of-the-art University of Tampa elevator was installed in the 1990s during one of the renovations to the building.

Originally, the Otis elevator was powered by a hydraulic system with water stored in rooftop tanks used to drive a rope-geared piston into a shaft, causing the elevator to rise and fall. That system was replaced with an electric motor in 1925. The annunciator was also replaced more recently, but otherwise the elevator has been preserved and looks today just as it would have to guests visiting the hotel.

The interior of the cab was given the same level of attention to detail as the rest of Plant's hotel, with ornately carved Cuban mahogany, coffered ceilings, and a brass cage door.

While the elevator is still capable of transporting passengers, it is seldom called upon to do so these days, and requires an attendant to operate it when it is in use. Visitors can enter the cabin, but those wishing to ascend in the height of Gilded Age style for themselves will need to wait for one of the infrequent occasions when the building's more modern elevator is out of commission for service.

According to Henry B. Plant Museum Curator Melissa Sullebarger, the oldest elevator in Florida is likely the one installed in St. Augustine's Ponce de Leon Hotel, which opened in 1888.

1891

Oldest Public Botanical Garden

Henry B. Plant Park

S Plant Ave., Tampa

The wonders awaiting visitors to the Tampa Bay Hotel were not confined within the 21 structures, but also surrounded them in the form of Plant Park. This, Tampa's oldest public botanical garden, was a popular place for hosting parties and hunting wild boar, which roamed in abundance. Its greenhouses provided fresh flowers for guests as well as herbs and spices for the hotel's kitchen. Occupying 60 acres along the Hillsborough River, its tropical plants and flowers were carefully selected by landscape designer Anton Fiehe. Interspersed are also important native flora, such as the Sabal palm (which became Florida's state tree in 1953) and Spanish bayonet plants, which were used to form a natural barrier around the park.

Undoubtedly, the garden's most famous tree is the DeSoto Oak, under the shade of which the Spanish explorer was said to have negotiated and bartered with the local tribes people. A tablet commemorating the event was placed under the tree by the De Soto Chapter of the DAR in 1929, but many historians have posited that "trade and treaties" represent a rather optimistic version of events. Rather, they contend that De Soto and his men more likely took what they wanted before destroying the village as they did elsewhere, in typical conquistador fashion.

This picture of the once-sprawling Henry B. Plant Park is from the Burgert Brothers collection. Photos courtesy of the Tampa-Hillsborough County Public Library System.

The garden features other firsts such as the area's oldest public artwork. Margaret Plant commissioned sculptor George Grey Barnard in 1900 to carve *Transportation* as an homage to her late husband's role in connecting Tampa to the rest of the world via train and steamship. Perched above the two figures and a strong box is an eagle—the logo of Plant's Southern Express Company.

To the garden's flora was added an equally diverse assortment of fauna. This included lizards, racoons, frogs, turtles, snakes, and gators that roamed freely, as well as enclosures that housed a resident bear and an aviary featuring exotic birds. From this sprang Tampa's first zoo in 1930, eventually relocating to its current location at Lowry Park in 1957.

There's no shortage of amazing botanical gardens in the area, including the Florida Botanical Gardens in Largo and the Marie Selby Botanical Gardens in Sarasota.

1894

Oldest Jewish Congregation

Congregation Schaarai Zedek

3303 W. Swann Ave., Tampa

It wasn't until 1763 that Jewish people were officially allowed to reside in Florida, although it is likely that some made their way to what would become the Sunshine State as conversos fleeing Spain and the rest of Europe. The first documented Jewish settlers in Tampa were Emaline Quentz Miley and her husband Bill, who settled in the Odessa area in 1844. Others began to arrive in numbers during and after the Civil War, as the Florida frontier presented new opportunities for merchants, shopkeepers, and entrepreneurs like Abe and Issac Maas who launched their Maas Brothers department store in 1886.

By 1890, there were more than 20 Jewish families living in Tampa. On October 14, 1894, 31 men and women gathered at the home of M. Henry Cohen and chose Schaarai Zedek ("Gates of Righteousness") as the name of the city's first Jewish congregation (and the fifth Jewish congregation in the state). Rabbi D. Jacobson served as the congregation's first spiritual leader when a synagogue was built in 1899 at 1205 Florida Avenue. The congregation also led the way in establishing the city's first Jewish social organization, Jewish women's organization, and Jewish cemetery.

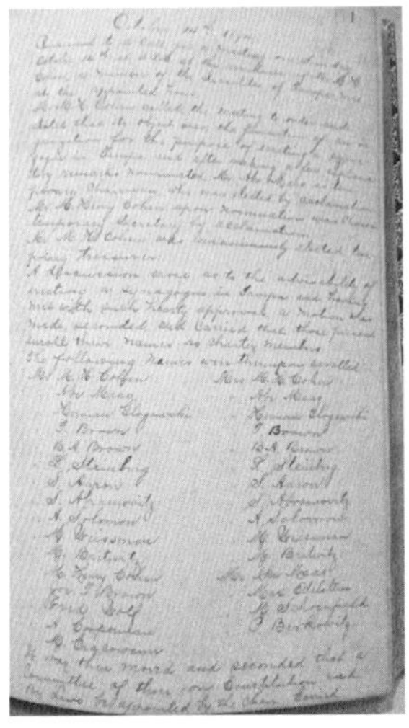

(Left) Meeting notes from October 14, 1894 detail the establishment of the area's first Jewish congregation. Photos courtesy of Congregation Schaarai Zedek. (Right) 1926 Burgert Brothers photo of Schaarai Zedek Temple at 510 South Delaware Ave, courtesy of the Tampa-Hillsborough County Public Library System.

In 1901 Jacobson was succeeded by Rabbi Friedman, whose more modern religious interpretations caused the orthodox-leaning members to split off, after which the congregation's constitution was amended to reflect that Reform Judaism would be their official form of worship.

In 1903 a second congregation, Rodeph Sholom, was established and is today the oldest Conservative Jewish congregation in the area. Rodeph Sholom's synagogue on Bayshore Boulevard, which was built in 1969, is also the oldest synagogue in Tampa.

Both congregations have continued to thrive, and dozens of others have been established since. Today, Rabbi Joel Simon provides leadership at Schaarai Zedek, (now located at 3303 W. Swann Avenue) to roughly 4,000 adults and children.

Tampa's first Jewish mayor, Herman Glogowski, laid the cornerstone when Schaarai Zedek's synagogue was built in 1899.

1896

Oldest Italian Market

Cacciatore Brothers

5610 Hanley Rd., Tampa

Ask any three residents what the area's largest and best-known Italian market is, and it wouldn't be uncommon for all three to respond with Mazzaro's. There's no denying that the coffee roasting business started 30 years ago by former Pittsburghers Sam and Pat Cuccaro has become essentially St. Petersburg's own one-block little Italy, complete with a deli, imported wines, meats, and cheeses, vintage Vespas, and home goods. Now try asking the same three individuals what the area's oldest Italian market is, and there will likely be far less consensus, if any responses at all. The answer can be found today in Tampa's Town 'n' Country neighborhood, though like so much of the area's Italian heritage, the story really begins in Ybor City.

When the last of the five Cacciatore brothers left Santo Stefano for Tampa in 1896, the others had already established a grocery store. Together the five brothers, Giuseppe, Ignazio, Silvestro, Filippo, and Salvatore opened a second storefront and meat

The deli counter in the market's current location comprises largely the same offerings as a century ago. Photo by the author.

Brothers Silvestro, Ignacio, and Fillipo, and Steve Cannella pose for the camera at Cacciatore Bros. market in Ybor City during the 1920s. Photo courtesy of Phillip Cacciatore.

market at 1816 7th Avenue. As the family and its business quickly grew in size and scope, it came to reflect the unique cultural heritage of Ybor—a mixture of Italian, Spanish, and Cuban. Among the first and second generations, those who were not employed in the family's own ventures often worked at one of the many cigar manufacturers.

From the business the five brothers founded, others emerged and spun off including Cacciatore Meat Packers, Frontier Meat Packers, and Cacciatore & Sons, which was formed in 1953 by Ignazio and his son Frank. As the Ybor City neighborhood declined, the original Cacciatore Brothers business relocated to its current address where it is now run by the third generation of the family.

For 126 years now the market has retained its distinctive flavor. In the more literal sense, that flavor comes from the family's original recipe for homemade Italian sausage, more than 60 varieties of cheese (including Locatelli pecorino, Auricchio provolone and parmesan Reggiano), and plenty of wines for pairing.

Many assume that scachatta (or scacciata), which is similar to tomato pie, is an Italian offering. Its combination of Sicilian and Cuban elements, though, makes it unique to Tampa.

1899

Oldest Electric Company

Tampa Electric Company (TECO)

702 N. Franklin St., Tampa

No doubt the extent to which many contemplate their electric provider begins and ends with the monthly bill, but in the case of TECO, its history as much as its generators qualify the business as a true powerhouse.

Founded in 1899, TECO was initially involved in powering Tampa's streetcars. It acquired Consumers Electric Light and Power, which lacked the finances to rebuild their dam on the Hillsborough River after it was blown up with dynamite in 1898 (though officially unsolved, the crime has been attributed to local cattlemen who took issue with the company). Under new ownership, the dam was rebuilt and produced power until 1933, when it was again destroyed (this time by a hurricane).

By 1906 TECO's first coal-fired steam generating plant was producing another stream of revenue for the company. In 1913, as electricity made its way into local homes, TECO came up with the bright idea to give away lightbulbs. A year later, modern offices were opened at Tampa and Cass streets.

In the 1920s electricity sales surged past trolley revenue as Tampa's population grew. In 1924 Peter O. Knight, who has been with the company since its founding, became president and held that post for 22 years. Knight's foresight in paying off the company's debts allowed it to weather the Great Depression. Knight is not the only significant local name connected to TECO

TECO's Big Bend Power Station as of March 2011, by Wknight94 licensed under CC BY-SA 3.0

during this time—it also employed as Director of Advertising one Francis Bellamy, author of the Pledge of Allegiance.

From 1946 to 1954 Francis Gannon served as the next president. He was followed by William MacInnes who shifted TECO's main source of power from oil to coal. To enable that change, TECO developed a barge network, which added shipping and transport to its diversified interests. H. L. Culbreath succeeded MacInnes in 1971 and focused on addressing environmental issues. During his tenure, the Big Bend Unit Four was completed in 1985 and a year later its discharge canal was made into a manatee sanctuary and viewing center.

In 1981 the company was restructured with TECO Energy as the holding company for all energy-related ventures and TECO Diversified as the umbrella for all other ventures. In the 2000s most of the company's seven principal subsidiaries were sold. Domestic ownership of the business came to an end in 2016, when TECO Energy was acquired by Nova Scotia-based Emera, Inc.

Presently, TECO serves over 800,000 customers with a coverage area of about 2,000 square miles across Hillsborough, Pinellas, Polk, and Pasco counties.

1902

Oldest Theater

Centro Asturiano de Tampa

1913 N. Nebraska Ave., Tampa

The Tampa Bay area has an abundance of historic theaters and event venues, not least of which is the Tampa Theatre, the local landmark and iconic movie palace designed by John Eberson in 1926. There's also the Meighen Theatre (now the Richey Suncoast Theatre), also built in 1925, where silent screen actor and New Port Richey resident Thomas Meighan famously flipped the switch to play the theater's first "talkie." The Nancy and David Bilheimer Capitol Theatre dates back to 1921, and the Asolo Repertory Theatre was originally built in Italy in the 18th century before Everett "Chick" Austin, as the first director of the John and Mable Ringling Museum of Art, acquired its interior in 1949 and had it transported and reconstructed in Sarasota.

The oldest continually operating theater and performance venue (original to the area) is almost certainly the one within the Centro Asturiano in Ybor City, which dates back to 1902. At the turn of the century, Ybor City was populated almost entirely by immigrants from Cuba, Spain, Italy, and elsewhere. Very much a world unto itself, this gave rise to the establishment of mutual aid societies—membership organizations which provided cultural and social activities as well as more practical support like healthcare, insurance, and cemeteries.

Like many of the historic buildings in Tampa, the design was by M. Leo Elliot. The original building burned down in the 1910s

This Burgert Brothers Image from November 10, 1923 shows Community Players actors on the stage of the theater in Centro Asturiano for their production of the play, Priscilla. *Photo courtesy of the Tampa-Hillsborough County Public Library System.*

(as did the original Cuban Club and Italian Club) and was rebuilt in 1914. At its height in the mid-20th century, the club had as many as 6,000 members, but that declined following the closure of the hospital in 1990. Today, the club consists of roughly 200 members.

The theater has seating for up to 1,000 and has hosted the famous Cuban composer and pianist Ernesto Lecuona among others. During the Great Depression, the Works Progress Administration (WPA) funded musicals and plays there. Today the club continues to host events there and also offers the theater as a venue for weddings, corporate functions, and similar activities.

Centro Asturiano de Tampa has another unique feature—it claims to have the world's longest marble onyx bar.

1905

Oldest Catholic Church

Sacred Heart Catholic Church

509 N. Florida Ave., Tampa

Sacred Heart Catholic Church on North Florida Avenue is distinctive for a number of reasons. Architecturally, the church is predominantly Romanesque with a 135-foot dome, solid oak doors and pews, a Carrara marble altar, and stained-glass windows made by the Mayer Company in Munich, Germany. While these features make the church unique visually, its history further sets it apart from other places of worship.

The current Sacred Heart Church, which was completed in 1905 and is Tampa's oldest Catholic church, is not the first house of worship to have stood at the location. In the early 1850s, property at Ashley Drive and Twiggs Street (and subsequently exchanged for land at Florida Avenue and Twiggs Street) was deeded for a Catholic church. A small frame church was constructed there in 1859 and named St. Louis Parish in honor of both Dominican Missionary Luis Cancer, who was martyred on the shores of Tampa Bay in 1549, and King Louis IX of France. The church thrived and was expanded in 1883, but a yellow fever outbreak from 1887 to 1888 took a heavy toll including the lives of three pastors in just one year.

To fill the void left by these outbreaks, Jesuits of the South assumed pastoral leadership and the church remained under their auspices until 2005. Plans to construct a new church were announced in 1897 as the city underwent a railroad-driven

(Left) Exterior of Sacred Heart Catholic Church. Photo by the author. (Right) Burgert Brothers photo from September 2, 1926 of the church's interior with ornamentation looking towards the altar. Photo courtesy of the Tampa-Hillsborough County Public Library System.

boom. Ground was broken on February 16, 1898, and seven years and $300,000 later the new church was complete.

From the church also sprang Jesuit High School in 1899, which was located there until 1956 when it moved to North Himes Avenue. Sacred Heart Academy was established (originally as an elementary school) just North of the Church in 1931. In 1975 Sacred Heart Academy began offering high school classes and did so until it closed in 2012.

In the early 2000s, the Jesuits began withdrawing from parish work in Florida. They officially relinquished Sacred Heart Church to the Franciscans on July 15, 2005, and Fr. Andrew Reitz, OFM became the first Franciscan pastor of the parish in January of the following year.

Another spectacular local church is Saint Nicholas Greek Orthodox Cathedral in Tarpon Springs. Those visiting during the annual Epiphany celebration should expect large crowds.

1904

Oldest Country Club

Tampa Yacht & Country Club

5320 Interbay Blvd., Tampa

By 1900 Tampa was one of Florida's largest and most prosperous cities with a population of over 15,000. One measure of that prosperity was in the growing number of affluent business owners and professionals.

In 1904 "Ye Mystic Krewe of Gasparilla" arrived during the May Day celebration to "capture the city" for the first time. That same year, a group of Tampa's prominent citizens and business professionals established the Tampa Yacht & Country Club as a place to mix and mingle, sail boats, and ride horses (and, perhaps, avoid running into costumed pirates). The first clubhouse was built in 1905 at a cost of $7,000 and served members until it burned down in 1929. It was rebuilt the

This 1911 Burgert Brothers photo shows the Tampa Yacht and Country Club from the water. Photo courtesy of the Tampa-Hillsborough County Public Library System.

following year and a barn and paddock were added in 1931, but the club was reduced to ash once again by a fire in 1938.

The club's third and current location was built in 1939 at a cost of $40,000. In 1960, the club joined with the other original 13 Florida West Coast yacht clubs between Tarpon Springs and Naples to establish the Florida Council of Yacht Clubs. Since then, the number of clubs has nearly tripled to 36 statewide, from Pensacola to Jacksonville to the Florida Keys.

The first tennis courts were installed at the club in 1961. The current marina space was approved by the membership and completed in 1967 with 31 covered slips, 50 open slips, and another 65 spaces of dry storage. The club underwent a complete marina overhaul in 2015 and 2016, adding fixed Ipe docks to the north and south sandwiching two floating docks. In 1991 a 35 by 75-foot swimming pool was constructed over the previous one. A new complex opened in October of 2000, to house the locker rooms, fitness center, nursey, saunas, steam rooms, and pro shop.

The club has become more inclusive over the years. Even the Gasparilla pirate krewes are now welcomed with open arms. It has become part of the annual Gasparilla tradition for the pirates to brunch at the club before sailing across the bay to seize the key to the city from the mayor.

The club became a Platinum Club of America in 2003 and a Platinum Club of the World in 2021. For members wanting to play golf, the club has reciprocal relationships with other nearby clubs.

1905

Oldest Restaurant

Columbia Restaurant

2117 E. 7th Ave., Tampa

The restaurant business is notoriously difficult even under the best of circumstances, but it can be particularly vulnerable to unexpected challenges like those that businesses face today related to the COVID-19 pandemic. In 1919 it was a different, but no less daunting problem confronting Cuban immigrant Casimiro Hernandez Sr.—Prohibition was going into effect the following year and would likely spell the end of the small corner café he had started in in 1905, unless he found a way to adapt. His solution was to partner with the restaurant, La Fonda, next door and expand his operation into a full-scale restaurant. This new version of Columbia Restaurant has gone on to become the oldest restaurant in Florida and the largest Spanish restaurant on earth.

In 1929 Casimiro Jr. took over the business from his father with a vision of expanding it. During the Great Depression in 1935 he decided, like his father, to take a risk and open the Don Quixote Room, which was the first air-conditioned dining room in Tampa and also featured an elevated dance floor.

Adela, the daughter of Casimiro Jr., left Tampa to train as a concert pianist at the Juilliard School of Music. She married a concert violinist named Cesar Gonzmart, and the couple returned to operate the restaurant together in 1953. This newest generation of owners encountered new challenges—namely the decline of Ybor City, where the restaurant was located.

Families gather for Spanish cuisine in the Patio Dining Room (left) and the Don Quixote Dining Room (right). Photos by the author.

Drawing on their background in music, they built a showroom, the Siboney Room, in 1956, and drew top-tier Latin talent to perform there. They also expanded into other locations, opening a Columbia Restaurant in Sarasota in 1959, which is also now the oldest restaurant in that city.

Richard and Casey, the sons of Adela and Cesar, continued to manage the multiple restaurants and opened additional locations throughout Florida. Today, the business is passing to their children—the family's fifth generation—who continue to innovate, diversify, and keep the family business going strong.

Other restaurants under the family's umbrella include the Goody Goody hamburger restaurants, farm-to-fork local gastropub Ulele, and Italian restaurant, Casa Santo Stefano, which opened in 2020.

1910

Oldest Public Playground

Anderson Park

802 S. Rome Ave., Tampa

Playgrounds trace their origin to Germany where Henry Barnard is credited with making the first concept sketch in 1848. Eleven years later, Manchester, England, took the next step forward in actually constructing the first playground. It took nearly three decades more for the concept to cross the pond, with the first US playground opening in 1887 at Golden Gate Park in San Francisco. In 1903, the first government-funded playground opened, in 1906 the Playground Association of America (PAA) was formed, and one year after that, playgrounds got a boost when President Theodore Roosevelt became an advocate.

In Tampa, it was the efforts of Kate Jackson that produced the area's first playground, Anderson Park, in 1910. She approached Mayor D. B. McKay and, per the historical marker at the park,

These images of Kate Jackson and her family home in Hyde Park are displayed inside the Kate Jackson Community Center. Photos courtesy of the City of Tampa Parks and Recreation Department.

"is entitled to credit for the acquisition of Tampa's first public playgrounds," and she contributed a "considerable sum of money to its equipment." The design of the park's center for kids (now Kate Jackson Community Center) is based on her own Hyde Park family home.

Jackson, the youngest of four siblings, was no stranger to mobilizing neighborhood and city improvement initiatives, among which the playground was just one of many. Her father, John Jackson, planned the city's streets as a federal surveyor before serving a term as acting mayor in 1861. Her brother Thomas also served two terms as the city's first native-born mayor. Despite not being able to hold office (or even vote), true to her motto, "agitate and educate," Kate found other means of serving as what some say was the best mayor Tampa never had.

Kate played a key role in establishing the Academy of the Holy Names in 1881, which is today Florida's oldest all-girls high school. In 1910, she founded the Tampa Civic Association and a year later, in a public speech, cataloged the city's needs such as clean water and sewage systems to improve public health and sanitation. Her many contributions (which also include women's rights and nature preservation) have earned her a well-deserved bust along the Tampa Riverwalk.

Visitors can pay their respects to Kate and her father at Myrtle Hill Memorial Park. Also buried there is circus performer Ildebrando Zacchini, who invented the human cannonball act.

1911

Oldest Golf Course

Rocky Point Golf Course

4151 Dana Shores Dr., Tampa

Many of the Tampa Bay area's early European settlers came from Scotland, bringing with them their families, the determination and skills to carve out a better life, and a passion for the game of golf, which originated in Scotland in the 15th century. It is likely that the very first game of golf ever played in the US took place in 1886 on the two greens and one long fairway built by Scotsman and first Sarasota Mayor John Gillespie.

Even though Gillespie's original course was sold and developed in 1924, a year after his death, he lived to see his beloved game take root—by the turn of the century, several courses had been established throughout the Sunshine State.

The oldest in Tampa (and one of the oldest statewide) was established in 1911 by the Tampa Automobile Club. Cigar industry strikes at the time delayed completion of both the golf links and clubhouse, but nonetheless, by 1912 golfers were playing the first nine holes and construction was finished the following year.

The course temporarily halted operations in 1942 when the US entered World War II. Barracks for prisoners of war were set up on the course as part of Drew Army Airfield, but the course still saw recreational use by servicemen stationed there. In 1953, the property was turned back over to the city and leased to J. S.

This Burgert Brothers photograph from May of 1921 shows men playing golf at Rocky Point Golf Course. Photo courtesy of the Tampa-Hillsborough County Public Library System.

Curly Hurtman, who reopened the course in 1954 with his wife Merle. In 1963, they added a third stretch of nine holes and when their lease on the land expired in 1978, they passed the property over to the Tampa Sports Authority, which had been established in 1965 to plan and manage the city's sports and recreational facilities.

Today, the Tampa Sports Authority still manages the course (along with Raymond James Stadium, Babe Zaharias Golf Course, and Rogers Park Golf Course). The course is an 18-hole, par-71 with four sets of tees. It underwent a $700,000 update in 2015, but still remains true to the simpler, gimmick-free design of Florida's early courses.

Here's another bit of local golf history—from 1945 through 1962 Dunedin Golf Club (designed by Donald Ross) was the home of the PGA.

1912

Oldest Train Station

Tampa Union Station

601 N. Nebraska Ave., Tampa

The Tampa Bay area evolved as a patchwork, and while the various neighborhoods, towns, and cities all shared a proximity to one another, they were often worlds apart—each the product of different influences. Downtown Tampa sprang up around the original Fort Brooke; Ybor City and West Tampa were driven by the cigar factories; and Tarpon Springs had the sponge industry; while lumber, citrus, and ranching all shaped other areas. Railroad tracks were like the stitches binding them all together.

Henry Plant's South Florida Railroad was the first to arrive in 1883 with stops in Ybor City and at his own Tampa Bay Hotel. The Seaboard Air Line and Tampa Northern Railroad both formed in 1900 and brought new major railways into the area, and numerous regional and local railways sprang up alongside them.

As a way to bring order from the chaos, *Tampa Tribune* publisher Wallace Stovall and businessman Peter Knight established the Union Station Company in 1911. J. F. Leitner from South Carolina was selected as the architect whose Italian Renaissance-style station opened to the public on May 15, 1912.

The station was not only a commercial success, but it also brought together for the first time many of the areas diverse industries and ethnicities. It would continue operation through the Great Depression and both World Wars, but it fell into

This image of Tampa Union Station was captured by the Burgert Brothers on October 15, 1952. Photo courtesy of the Tampa-Hillsborough County Public Library System.

disrepair beginning in the 1970s and closed in 1984.

For many historic buildings that would have been the end of the line, but in 1988 a group of train enthusiasts and preservationists joined together under the banner of Tampa Union Station Preservation & Redevelopment Inc. After 10 years and four million dollars in restoration, the station was ready to welcome passengers once more. Starting in 2011 those passengers arrived in numbers enough to make it Amtrak's third busiest station in the state by 2017.

In 2009, it became the subject of Tampa Poet Laureate James E. Tokley Senior's "The Epic of Tampa Union Station," and three years later, the station marked its centennial year by being added to the National Register of Historic Railroad Landmarks.

Outside of the station is William C. Culbertson's public artwork titled Tampa Centennial Keep*—a 28-foot clock tower which depicts the station's history*

1912

OLDEST BAKERY

ALESSI BAKERY

2909 W. Cypress St., Tampa

When he arrived in Tampa from Sicily in 1912, Nicolo Alessi's single greatest asset was his skill in baking European-style baked goods. From the small bakery he opened initially on Cherry Street, he began to develop a reputation for the quality of his Italian and Cuban bread. In the early days, Nicolo used a horse and wagon to make deliveries.

Nicolo's son John inherited his father's business and passion, with numerous cake decorating awards to his credit. He continued to perfect his family recipes and eventually passed the business on to his own son, Phil, who had ideas for expanding the bakery. In 2008 he opened a $20 million, 100,000-square-foot plant off of Waters Avenue in Tampa's Town 'n' Country neighborhood. The new facility gave Alessi the ability to compete with larger supermarket bakeries, some of which, like Publix, now carry as many as 150 of Alessi's baked goods.

Founder Nicolo (far right) and his son John Alessi (second from right) are shown in this photo along with family and bakery staff. Photo courtesy of Jason Alessi.

Jason Alessi, seen here behind the bakery counter, represents the fourth generation to manage the family business. Photo by the author.

With the bakery growing to match Phil's vision, he decided to add a side business. In 1967 he started Alessi Promotions to promote and manage local boxers. Marvin Hagler and Joe Frazier are just a couple of the names to have fought on Alessi's boxing cards.

Phil Alessi Sr. passed away in 2018, but not before leaving the bakery and promotion businesses to his son, Phil Jr. Ownership changed once more and today Jason Alessi represents the fourth generation of the family to run the bakery. While he has worked behind the counter for more than 20 years, some of the bakery's employees have been there longer; for over half a century in some cases. According to Jason, the familial culture has been crucial in retaining staff during what some call "the great resignation." One member of the talented team who continues to construct mouthwatering marvels is Melissa Maggiore, who has appeared on national television and baked for an impressive list of celebrities, of which Joan Jett, Jon Bon Jovi, Megan Trainor, George Steinbrenner, and Taylor Swift are just the icing on top.

Alessi produces a variety of Tampa-centric treats including guava turnovers and scachatta, but credit for inventing "Cuban bread" belongs to La Segunda Bakery, which opened in 1915.

1915

Oldest High-Rise Building

Old Tampa City Hall

315 E. Kennedy Blvd., Tampa

Given the precision required by architecture and construction, it might surprise some to learn that there is considerably less precision when it comes to architectural terminology—at least in the case of what exactly constitutes a "high-rise." Beyond a tall modern building consisting of many floors, there isn't universal consensus. For the purpose of this chapter, however, let's apply the International Building Code (IBC) version, which defines a high-rise as having "an occupied floor more than 75 feet above the lowest level of fire department vehicle access."

This definition excludes the six-story Florida Brewing Company Building which was built in 1896 and, at 75 feet, remains the tallest building in

A bird's eye view of old Tampa City Hall, taken by the Burgert Brothers in 1916. Photo courtesy of the State Archives of Florida, Florida Memory.

Ybor City. The Citizens Bank Building, which was erected in 1913 and reached a height of 145 feet, was probably the first to meet the IBC's high-rise definition and would be the subject of this chapter had it not been demolished in 1978.

The next logical choice, rising 10 stories and 160 feet tall, is the Old Tampa City Hall. The building's eclectic design, often likened to a square layer cake, was that of architects Bonfoey and Elliott with structural drawings provided by H. G. Perring Engineering Company. It features Doric columns, detailed terra cotta work, and a balustrade. A seven-story tower rises from the first layer, with several ornamental heads alleged to have been fashioned from the visage of a Seminole Indian maiden. The top two stories of the building compose the bell and clock tower, from which hangs the 2,840-pound, four-sided clock donated by W. H. Beckwith Jewelry Company and known as "Hortense the Beautiful" for Hortense Ford, socialite and daughter of Dr. Louis Sims Oppenheimer, in recognition of her efforts to have the clock installed there.

McGucken and Hyer Contractors constructed the building at a cost of $235,000 using poured in place concrete post and beam on concrete bell footings. The building was completed and occupied in 1915 and remained Tampa's tallest structure until the Floridan Hotel was built in 1926. It was added to the US National Register of Historic Places in 1974.

Sarasota's Historic Palm Tower calls itself that city's first "skyscraper," but given that it has just seven stories, it probably better fits the IBC definition of "high-rise."

1916

Oldest Bicycle Shop

Joe Haskins Bike Shop (formerly Tampa Cycle)

2310 N. Florida Ave., Tampa

"A grease monkey with a heart of gold," an "angel in disguise," and "a giant of a man" represent just a few of the many fond descriptions of the man whose eponymous bike shop has been a hub for the local cycling community for over a century.

The story begins when Joe's uncle opened Tampa Cycle Shop in 1916. Haskins was born 15 years later in 1941, one of seven siblings, and honed his skills as a bike mechanic at the Mary Help of Christians Trade School. In 1958, at the age 17, he purchased his uncle's shop. The store cycled through a number of locations before it came to a halt at its present address in Tampa Heights in the mid-1970s. Haskins watched the neighborhood around him grow, deteriorate, gentrify, and undergo a second boom in growth that as of today has yet to slow down.

Through all of the changes though, Haskins developed deep lifelong relationships with residents and fellow biking enthusiasts. It's impossible to know how many bikes he provided on layaway plans or just outright gave away to those who were down on their luck. Nor is it known just how many awards and recognitions he was presented with over the years. With a wrench in hand and a smile on face, Haskins preferred to focus on doing what he loved most, which was building, repairing, and riding bicycles. He continued to work through the death of his first wife, Dorothy,

Joe Haskins' Bike Shop has seen the Tampa Heights neighborhood change around it more than once since it opened its doors there in the mid 1970s. Photo by the author.

and his son Kenneth. In 2012 he was married again to Michelle Calogne, who had been a bike mechanic at the shop and friend since she and her son moved to the neighborhood in 1978.

When Haskins lost a long battle against kidney disease on March 20, 2021, the community was devastated as demonstrated by the massive outpouring of condolences and personal stories that were shared online and elsewhere. Michelle now handles the stores operation and plans to keep it going well into the future, staying the course that her late husband mapped out so many years before.

The next step after procuring a bike is finding a place to ride it. A few popular options include the Pinellas Bike Trail, the Selmon Greenway, and Bayshore Boulevard.

1922

Oldest Radio Station

WDAE (AM 620/FM 95.3)

4002 W. Gandy Blvd., Tampa, FL

Commercial broadcasting began after World War I, but it didn't fully arrive until the KDKA broadcast of the 1920 presidential election results. Those operating radios were among the first to hear the news of Warren G. Harding's landslide victory over James M. Cox.

Newspapers took notice and when the *Tampa Daily Times* was approached by Harold McClung, who offered to sell them his broadcast equipment, they agreed to it.

The result was WDAE, which received authorization to broadcast on May 15, 1922. It was not the first in Florida to receive such authorization—WCAN in Jacksonville had received authorization one week earlier—but WDAE was the first to broadcast. This makes it, according to a letter from the FCC on the occasion of WDAE's 50th

The WDAE radio tower, photographed by the Burgert Brothers. Photo courtesy of the State Archives of Florida, Florida Memory.

birthday, the "First radio station to begin operations in the state of Florida."

The station's first studio consisted of a small room with a wall microphone and transmitting equipment in an adjacent room inside of what was then the Citrus Exchange Building (now the Maas Brothers Building) along with broadcasting equipment on the roof. In April of 1922 air tests were the conducted under the guidance of W. R. McDonald and G. C. Warner—both experienced radio operators who had been recruited to operate the station. On Monday, May 15, WDAE first signed on, broadcasting at 833 kilocycles. Locals with their own sets listened in at the request of the *Times* between seven and nine pm to see what they could hear, which were baseball scores and phonograph records.

Initially, WDAE broadcasted on multiple frequencies but by 1941, it had settled on AM 1250. In 1947 it added an FM station. Throughout the 1940s and 1950s, the Golden Age of Radio, the stations aired news, sports, operas, gameshows, comedies, and big band music. In the 1960s, the FM station switched to mostly instrumental "beautiful music" while the AM station played Top 40 hits. The station continued to change with the times, to oldies in the 1980s, classic country in 1994, and sports radio in 1999 with the acquisition by Clear Channel Communications (now iHeartMedia).

According to the historical marker at the corner of Zack and Franklin streets, Mayor Charles H. Brown referred to radio broadcasting as "The Wonder of the Age."

1923

Oldest Streetcar

Birney #163

As early as 1885, Tampa had a local rail system which ran between Ybor City and Tampa. Both the Consumers Electric Light and Power Company and the Tampa Street Railway and Power Company operated steam-powered cars until 1893, when Tampa Street Railway converted to electric. This started a pricing war from which Consumers emerged victorious, driving its competitor out of business and giving Consumers a monopoly on supplying electricity to Tampa. Consumers also acquired the Tampa and Palmetto Beach Railway before it, in turn, was absorbed into Tampa Electric Company (TECO) in 1899, which continued to maintain the 21.5 miles of track with stops in Ybor City, West Tampa, DeSoto Park, and Ballast Point.

The lighter weight "Birney Car" invented in 1915 by Charles Birney and Joseph Bosenbury became the model of choice nationwide. Of the roughly 2,000 such cars produced between 1914 and the late 1920s, one of these was Birney #163, running on the TECO line from 1923 until service ended in 1946.

At that point Birney #163's story goes off the rails, so to speak. The car was sold to a homeowner in Sulphur Springs for use as a small vacation cabin. There it fell into disuse until Jeanne MacNeill Mydelski acquired the property in 1978. Even though her plan to convert the Birney into an office for her travel agency became cost prohibitive, she continued to preserve it. In 1991 she donated it to the Tampa Trolley Society, which restored it as part

The interior of a Birney street car. Burgert Brothers photo courtesy of the State Archives of Florida, Florida Memory.

of its objective to reintroduce trolley service between downtown Tampa and Ybor City. Resurrecting Birney #163 entailed over 10,000 volunteer hours spent restoring the ash wood on the roof, oak flooring, cherry wood seats, and mahogany for the wall panels, doors, and window frames.

In 2002, under Mayor Dick Greco, the initial heritage line was opened, and streetcars once again transported passengers around the area. The line is currently managed by HART with 11 stops from Centennial Park to Whiting, and from time to time, some lucky passengers get to ride on Birney #163, which is now one of less than 30 of its model still in existence and the oldest restored streetcar operating in Florida.

Tampa is also home to the oldest operating tugboat in Florida, Dorothy, *which was built in 1898 and helps pull the Gasparilla pirate ship across the bay each year.*

1924

Oldest Facility Specifically Designed as Senior Housing

Old People's Home

1203 E. 22nd Ave., Tampa

Among the stigmas often attached to the Sunshine State is that of being America's retirement capital, and it's true (according to Consumer Affairs) that as of 2022, Florida has the largest percentage of senior citizens (at 21%). But that image lodged in the American collective consciousness of masses of seniors playing shuffleboard, pickleball, and bridge together in the common areas of specially designed communities would likely have been puzzling to Tampa Bay area residents throughout the first quarter of the 20th century, prior to the creation of the Old People's Home.

When the area's first home specifically designed for the care of the elderly was opened in 1924, it represented an achievement both for those receiving and those overseeing that care. Whereas men in those days typically called the shots as far as the operation of such facilities, the original bylaws laid out by the all-woman board of managers limited male involvement to the roles of trustees and advisors. Even Peter O. Knight, who donated the 4.5 acres on which the home was built, was restricted from holding office within (although the park there, with its benches, gazebos,

The iron front gate and columned portico of the Old People's Home, current operated as the Home Association, Inc. Photo by TampAGS, for AGS Media licensed under CC BY-SA 3.0.

oak-tree canopy, and shuffleboard court, was named Sarah Knight Park in honor of his mother).

The two-story building itself was designed by Frank A. Winn Jr. and A. H. Johnson with Colonial Revival style for the main facade. In addition to the bedrooms, the *Tampa Tribune* reported it as having a reception area, kitchen, dining room, and four sun parlors on the first floor and an infirmary, two wards, and baths on the second floor. It was also equipped with elevators, refrigeration, and running water in all of the bedrooms.

The building has since changed its name (to The Home Association), but its mission remains the same—it continues to operate as a not-for-profit senior skilled-nursing facility.

The name Peter O. Knight comes up often when digging into local history. In addition to being a former TECO president, he also served six years as Hillsborough's state attorney.

1926

OLDEST RACETRACK

TAMPA BAY DOWNS

11225 Race Track Rd., Tampa

Opened in 1926 as Tampa Downs, the only thoroughbred racetrack on Florida's Gulf Coast is also one of the oldest and most well-maintained racetracks in America. It was originally established as the racetrack for the West Coast Jockey Club by Harvey Myers, an Ohio Investor, and Kentucky Colonel Martin "Matt" J. Winn, who had served as President of Churchill Downs racetrack. The inaugural card featured a veritable "who's who" of sports celebrities including Babe Ruth, Jack Dempsey, and Gene Sarazen, as well as big top bigwig John Ringling.

Despite the track's success out of the starting block, attendance suffered during the Great Depression and again during World War II, when the track was inactive for several years before finding new use in 1943 as a jungle-warfare training facility for the US Army.

Following the war, the track's "modern era" began in 1947 with a new owner, attorney Frank Hobbs, and a new name, "Sunshine Park." During this period, a number of famous sportswriters became regulars there including Red Smith, Arthur Daley, Fred Russell, and Grantland Rice, who called it the "Santa Anita of the South."

In the 1980s the track was renamed Tampa Bay Downs and launched into a state of continual improvement. A seven-furlong chute was added to the one-mile dirt "Oldsmar Oval" in 1984,

Crowds watch from the seats in the grandstands and on the track in these 1926 Burgert Brothers photographs. Photos courtesy of the Tampa-Hillsborough County Public Library System.

and a seven-eighths-mile turf course was completed in 1998. The Clubhouse was remodeled in 1999, the Downs Golf Practice Facility was opened in 2003, and the Silks Poker Room launched that same year. The Trakus electronic tracking system was installed in 2011.

Just a few of the track's most memorable moments include:

- In 1981 apprentice jockey Julie Krone won her first career race at the track, before going on to become a US Racing Half of Famer;
- In 2007, Carl Nafzger's 3-year-old Street Sense achieved a win before going on to do the same at the Kentucky Derby; and
- William Mott selected Tampa Bay downs for the 2011 starts for his Royal Delta, who would twice win the Breeders' Cup Distaff, and his Drosselmeyer, who won the Breeders' Cup Classic.

Visitors won't see any Greyhound racing—Florida banned it in 2018. Since then, groups like the Gulf Coast Chapter of Gold Coast Greyhound Adoptions have found the dogs new homes.

1927

OLDEST HOSPITAL

TAMPA GENERAL HOSPITAL

1 Tampa General Cir., Tampa

Prior to the 1920s, Davis Islands had yet to be created atop what was then just two swampy mounds (Little Grassy Key and Big Grassy Key), and the area's medical needs were met first by the two-story Tampa General Hospital and subsequently, beginning in 1910, by the 32-bed Gordon Keller Memorial Hospital on North Boulevard. In 1925 a $1 million bond issue was approved to construct a new medical facility on the man-made island which had been recently created by D. P. Davis. Local lore has it that the hospital's location was decided on the Palma Ceia Country Club golf course where Davis was playing with Mayor Chancey, James Swann, and Dr. H. Brown Farrior.

This photo by the Burgert Brothers, dated March 14, 1958, shows Tampa General Hospital from the Platt Street Bridge. Photo courtesy of the Tampa-Hillsborough County Public Library System.

Construction of the new 250-bed Tampa Municipal Hospital began in 1926, and the following year patients were relocated there from Gordon Keller. In 1928 the City of Tampa acquired the hospital which Nurse Clara C. Frye had established in her home as a healthcare facility for black patients. Clara continued working there at what was renamed Tampa Negro Hospital until she retired. In 1937 the city opened a new 62-bed hospital for black patients and named it Clara Frye Memorial Hospital. This hospital was eventually absorbed into the hospital on Davis Islands, which, in 1956, was renamed Tampa General Hospital.

In 1970 the hospital and the University of South Florida College of Medicine signed an affiliation agreement which made Tampa General the primary teaching hospital for the university's med school and residency programs. In 1979 a $14.2 million renovation and expansion was completed. The following decades saw further changes with the opening of a 59-bed rehabilitation center in 1984, the opening of the West Pavilion in 1986, the addition of a helipad in 1989, and the opening of a Children's Medical Center in 1992. The multi-phased, multi-unit Bayshore Pavilion first opened in 2007.

Today, Tampa General Hospital is a veritable city unto itself with 1,041 beds and more than 8,000 team members. It is one of the region's only university-level academic medical centers and features the only ACS designated level 1 adult and pediatric trauma center in the Tampa Bay area.

Tampa General Hospital is also one of only three burn centers in Florida and one of the country's leading organ transplant centers as well.

1928

Oldest Airfield

Tampa International Airport (Formerly Drew Field)

4100 George J. Bean Pkwy., Tampa

At the beginning of the 20th century, aviation was in its infancy. The Wright Flyer made its historic flight in 1903 and a decade later, on the first day of 1914, Tony Jannus completed the first regularly scheduled commercial flight between St. Petersburg and Tampa. Savvy developer John H. Drew saw an opportunity in creating a private landing field on land he acquired from Hugh C. Macfarlane. The resulting Drew Field would take an indirect route to becoming Tampa International Airport.

The City of Tampa, also recognizing the value of an airport, signed a five-year lease with Drew for use of the field. The deal gave the city the option to buy, while Drew received the gas and oil concessions. The quality of the field, however, was problematic, and there was a push to build a new airport on a man-made island off of Ballast Point by those seeking to entice Pan Am to make Tampa its headquarters.

The city council became deadlocked, Pan Am made Miami its home, and development at Drew Field stalled until it became a source of depression-era work projects. The city purchased the land once the lease expired in 1934 and by 1938, Drew Field had become one of the top-rated fields in the state. Meanwhile, in 1935, the Peter O. Knight Airport opened on Davis Islands from which National and Eastern Airlines operated until 1946.

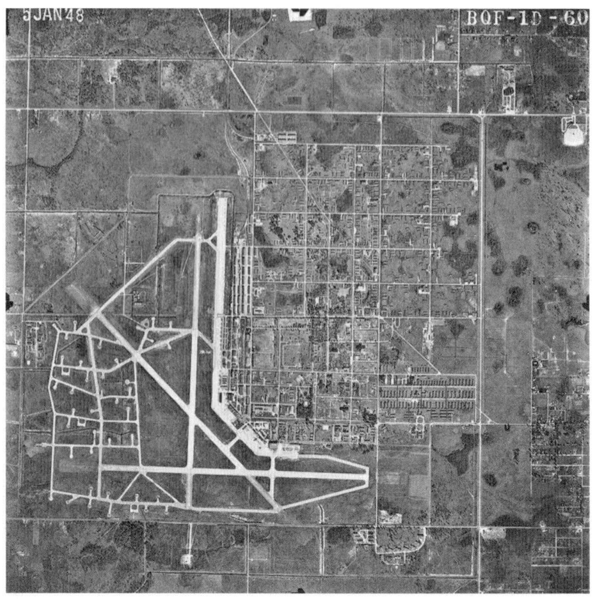

This aerial photo taken in 1948 shows Drew Field in its World War II military configuration. Photo by the United States Geological Survey, public domain.

With war looming, in 1940 the army leased Drew Field, which it expanded and modernized for use as a sub post and training center. In 1946, the army relinquished the airfield to the federal government, which in turn deeded most of it to the Aviation Authority and Tampa airline operations, at which point it was renamed Tampa International Airport. In 1952 a new terminal was opened and by 1961, it was serving more than a million passengers annually. To alleviate congestion, construction of a new Landside/Airside terminal began in 1968 and was completed in 1971.

The old terminal was demolished in 1975—the place where it once stood is now a private jet port.

1928

Oldest Preserved Rooming House

The Bing Rooming House Museum

205 Allen St., Plant City FL 33563

The many opulent hotels that sprang up along the Gulf Coast in the years between the arrival of the railroads and Great Depression typically meant little to black travelers—the "separate but equal" doctrine adopted as a result of the 1896 *Plessy v. Ferguson* trial required them to seek accommodations elsewhere. In 1936 Victor Green published the first edition of his Negro Motorist's Guide (a.k.a., the Green Book) to help black travelers find hospitable lodging, just like the rooming house owned and operated by Janie Wheeler Bing.

Janie Wheeler was born in 1889 and raised by her mother after her father was killed in a railway accident. She earned a teaching certificate in 1917 and planned to pursue a career in education in Miami, but fate intervened in the form of Elijah L. Bing, with whom she fell in love and married.

As of this time, the Bing Rooming House Museum is open by appointment. Photo by the author.

Janie stayed in Plant City and raised three children while managing her Bing Rooming House, which was built in 1928, to which she added the Seminole Restaurant in 1931. From there in the Laura Street African American Business district, she hosted a wide range of black travelers and professionals including doctors, entertainers, teachers, and Negro League baseball players. Even though "separate but equal" was struck down on paper by the 1954 *Brown V. Board of Education* case, she kept the rooming house in operation until 1975.

Janie's son, Elijah Lutrell Bing Jr., continued in his mother's footsteps as an educator, receiving a degree in biology from Florida A&M University and a master's degree in education from Columbia University after serving in World War II. He returned to Plant City to become a principal at Glover Elementary and Marshall High School before becoming the assistant superintendent for supportive services for Hillsborough County Schools until 1978.

Janie's grandson, Jimmy Washington, recognized the importance of preserving the family legacy and undertook efforts to have the rooming house recognized as a historic landmark, which came to fruition in 2002. Renovated to serve as a museum, today it preserves Plant City's African American history.

Those seeking more information on the area's black history can find a PDF version of the Florida Black Heritage Trail here: https://files.floridados.gov/media/32347/blackheritagetrail.pdf.

1933

Oldest Family-Owned Jewelers

Hayman Jewelry Co.

305 E. Madison St., Tampa

The same year that Haslam's opened in St. Petersburg, Solomon "Sol" Hayman was starting his own jewelry business. Born in 1907 and no stranger to tough times and hard work, Sol was a fifth generation Tampa native (his great grandmother had moved there in the 1850s, decades before the city's population reached four digits). When Sol was five years old his father died of tuberculosis, which meant that after completing the third grade, Sol and his brother went to work at Parker's farm. Their tasks included squeezing the juice from sugarcane and pumping it upstairs into a barn.

In his twenties, Sol went to work for a local jeweler. His mother had remarried a cigar roller and together they had six children in addition to Sol and his brother and sister from his mother's first marriage. In 1933 at the age of 26, Sol borrowed $500 from a local doctor and began selling jewelry from his car. Six years later he had a storefront on Franklin where he and all eight of his siblings joined him. During this time, the store often stayed open until 11 p.m. to catch the crowds coming from the theaters downtown.

In the 1940s, Hayman's also began selling small appliances and electronics such as toasters and clock radios, to which they added televisions in the 1950s. They hired repairman Earl McGriff (whose son, Fred, became a major league baseball player who ended his career as a Tampa Bay Ray with 493 homeruns), and a team of up to 23 outside sales associates.

Sol's son, Dan, entered the business in 1965 and became a partner when Sol passed away 14 years later. By 1985 Dan had bought out his aunt and uncle, moved to a new location on Franklin next to the Maas Brothers department store, and carved off the appliance business. In 1990, the store moved to its current location, which had been a ticket office for Eastern Airlines. Since then, both of Dan' daughters, who are certified gemologists, have joined the company. Dan himself is a master jeweler and continues to work at the store part-time.

Those with a taste for southwestern-styled jewelry should check out the collection on display in the Jewel Box within the James Museum of Western and Wildlife Art.

Dan Hayman behind the counter of his family's store. Photo by the author.

1941

Oldest Nudist and Naturist Resort

Lake Como Family Nudist Resort & Community

20500 Cot Rd., Lutz, FL 33558

Fashion can serve as a means of tracing cultural and social change. Take women's swimwear for example, which evolved from long bathing gowns to more fitted outfits in the 19th century, then into the bikini (introduced in 1946) and more recently the thong, as the trend continues toward exposing ever more skin. Even "next to nothing," for some, however, just isn't close enough; hence, the proliferation of nudist and naturalist resorts in the Tampa Bay area (specifically Pasco County, the self-proclaimed "Nudist Capital of the World," with dozens of such communities).

The nudist, or "back to nature" movement first arrived in the US in the 1920s, led by Kurt Barthel, and followed the sun and warm weather south. It arrived in the town of Lutz in 1941 when

These 1961 photos shows community members enjoying an afternoon by the lake. Photo Courtesy of Lake Como Family Nudist Resort.

the Lake Como Resort opened with the mission "to preserve and promote our family nudist lifestyle and community, establish a positive image with government and community leaders, and cultivate our natural beauty while promoting environmental responsibility as a legacy for our future generations."

That part about "a positive image with government and community leaders" has met with mixed success over the years. The resort was given a boost when *The Garden of Eden* was filmed there in 1954. In 1961, however, then-owner of the resort Art "Cot" Coterill was jailed for defying a state law forcing nudists to comply with a bevy of new requirements including permits, submitting to fingerprinting, and listing all prior criminal convictions. The Florida Supreme Court overturned the statute in 1962 and Cot was released back to the community, which named him "Outstanding Nudist of the Year." By the end of that decade, Lake Como had become the largest nudist club in America and the first with over 3,000 members.

In the 1980s the community installed a hot tub, swimming pool, and open-air tiki bar (today known as the "Butt Hutt"). More recently, in the 1990s, the resort reincorporated as Lake Como Co-Op to offer ownership to new members, thus accommodating those wanting more "skin in the game," so to speak.

For those who want the full history of nudism laid bare, the American Nudist Research Library is located not too far away in Kissimmee, Florida.

1949

Oldest Bar

The Hub Bar

719 N. Franklin St., Tampa

The question of which of the area's bar qualifies as the oldest gets muddled rather quickly. The Tiny Tap Tavern, for instance, started out as a gas station in the 1930s, but didn't officially begin pouring beers until 1951. The Hub Bar, on the other hand, has been serving up cocktails for at least 71 years, though it may be even older than that.

When the *Tampa Bay Times* undertook to distill the Hub's official history in 2019, they discovered a Hub Hotel listed in the city directory as early as 1933, though it is unclear if it included a bar. There was apparently a Hub Saloon located at 801 Tampa Street from 1935 until 1943, during which time it passed through three separate owners. There was also a bar called the Hub in Ybor City listed in 1947.

None of these, however, are known to be connected to the current Hub, which was established in 1949 by Pio Guerra Jr. at 901 N. Florida Avenue, the site of his Elite Cigar Store. Pasquale Deyoria purchased the bar from Guerra in 1956. Meanwhile, popular pianist Klink Lemmon entertained patrons throughout the 1950s.

Over the next few decades, the composition of the neighborhood changed and the Hub added to its affluent business patrons a mix of blue collar workers and the University of Tampa crowd.

The Hub Bar has been serving up potent drinks for more than seven decades. Photo by the author.

In 2002 the building's owners (First Presbyterian Church) let the Hub know it was closing time, as they planned to demolish the structure in favor of a parking lot. The Hub rolled on down the street to its current location, where it has continued the "dive bar" style it embraced in the 1980s.

The bar's current co-owners, Charles Fox and Ferrell "Skooter" Melton, are reluctant to officially call their bar the oldest in Tampa or the Tampa Bay Area. What they will commit to is serving drinks with enough of a punch that after just a couple most individuals have trouble remembering their own age, let alone that of the bar.

For those seeking more of an open air style dive bar, consider visiting Mahuffer's in Indian Shores, which evolved (somewhat) from being a bait shop.

1954

Oldest Ice Cream Parlor

Bo's Ice Cream

7101 N. Florida Ave., Tampa

Kenneth Miller Bosanko, born around 1907 in Oklahoma, served in World War II and in the US Coast Guard before becoming a purchasing agent and raising a family. Things might have been perfect except for one little thing that kept bothering him: however hard he searched, he just wasn't satisfied with the quality of the local ice cream. Eventually, in the "do it yourself" spirit that his generation is known for, he moved to Tampa and started his own ice cream stand in 1954.

Things were tough at first; the cost of a cone was a dime and the menu consisted of just a few basic flavors. Bosanko, or "Mr. Bo" as he was known, had to sell greeting cards as a side hustle to keep the wheels of his business churning. He stuck with it and weathered the ups and downs of the Seminole Heights neighborhood where he started, eventually becoming a local institution. Even so, in the '70s and '80s when the neighborhood became a haven for drug dealers, Bosanko's son, Kenny, recalls having to chase off would-be robbers with guns of their own and destroying a matchbox of crack cocaine a dealer had stashed in their parking lot.

Mr. Bo passed control of the business to his son Bob, who had been working there alongside his father since he was eight years

Locals line up at the counter of Bo's Ice Cream to keep the heat at bay. Photo by the author.

old. When Bob passed away in 1992, his brother Kenny stepped in to operate the shop. Kenny passed the business on to his daughter, Tammy Vitte, and she in turn passed it on to her son, who is now the fourth generation to own the family business.

Today Seminole Heights is experiencing something of a renaissance fueled by the latest wave of new residents, and from its simple blue facade at the corner of Florida Avenue and East Flora Street, Bo's continues to help Tampanians new and old beat the heat. The menu has expanded to include a variety of floats, milkshakes, and sundaes (including the upside-down banana split which has become a perennial favorite).

A newer trend in the area has been alcohol-infused ice cream. The first shop to do so was St. Petersburg's Beans & Barlour, which opened in 2018.

1954

Oldest Family-Owned Premium Cigar Factory

J.C. Newman Cigar Company

2701 N. 16th St., Tampa

In 1886 the Sanchez y Haya cigar company became the first to roll cigars in what would become Ybor City. It was joined by other cigar makers brought to the area by Vicente Martinez Ybor, Ignacio Haya, and Hugh Macfarlane in the late 1800s, giving Tampa the nickname "Cigar City" which, at its height, employed as many as 10,000 workers rolling 500 million cigars annually. Save for Arturo Fuente, none of those original local manufacturers remain. Some floundered following worker strikes, while others were unable to compete with more cost-efficient machine-made cigars and the introduction of mass-produced cigarettes. Their old factory buildings have been occupied by newer arrivals, repurposed, or demolished.

There is, however, one name that might have been familiar to Tampa's first wave of cigar manufacturers: Julius Caeser Newman, who began rolling cigars in 1895 at his family barn in Cleveland, Ohio. At the age of 14 he became a cigarmaker's apprentice and then a journeyman, but employment became scarce following a recession and he decided to launch his own business.

J. C. Newman's first brand of cigars was called "A. B. C." (for the local streetcar line Akron, Bedford, and Cleveland). In 1927 the company merged with Mendelsohn to become M & N Cigar

Images of the factory and clocktower known today as "El Reloj," courtesy of J.C. Newman Cigar Company.

Manufacturers. Newman's sons joined the business after World War II and decided to relocate their operations to Tampa in 1954. In celebration of their 100th anniversary in 1995, the company reverted to its original name, J. C. Newman Cigar Co.

The company's building in Ybor is known as "El Reloj" for the four-sided clock atop its seven-story brick tower, but it is not the first building in town to have been known by that name. El Reloj once referred to the cigar factory in West Tampa that served both Pendas y Alvarez and Regensburg.

Now in its fourth generation of ownership, J. C. Newman continues to use traditional hand-rolled techniques to produce their cigar brands which include Cuesta-Rey, Diamond Crown, and La Unica. It is considered the oldest family-owned premium cigar maker in Tampa and in the entire United States.

A newer wave of handmade cigar businesses has returned to Ybor over the years, including both King Corona Cigars and Tabanero Cigars.

1958

Oldest Bowling Alley

Pin Chasers

5555 W. Hillsborough Ave., Tampa

The 1950s are often viewed as a prosperous time in American history (although prosperity, then as now, was not always evenly distributed or accessible to all). The burgeoning middle class spilled out into the suburbs. Rock and roll replaced big band on the radio, television was new, and poodle skirts were a thing. In 1958 Eisenhower was president, the hula hoop had just been introduced, and a 15-year-old Bill Morris was desperate to find a way to keep cool in the sweltering summer heat.

He found relief in the Regal Lanes bowling alley, where he discovered that the better he bowled, the more free games he could accrue and the longer he could enjoy the establishment's air conditioning. One day, the Palazzolos, who owned the bowling alley, offered Morris some money after he helped sweep up sawdust from contractors working on the lanes. Morris kept coming back and occasional chores turned into a job and then a career.

By 1976, it seemed to the Palazzolos that their business had "jumped the shark" a year before Arthur Fonzarelli did so on the show *Happy Days*. They passed ownership to Morris, who set about developing partnerships with others in and outside of the bowling industry. Former general manager Greg Pietz credits a relationship with Maryland Fried Chicken as being key to turning the business around.

Shown here is the entrance to the Veteran's location—one of three Pin Chasers bowling alleys. Photo by the author.

To Morris, keeping the business classy meant more than the coats and ties his staff wore. It meant managing a working-class country club open to all regardless of age, gender, color, or creed. This included hosting the area's first all-black bowling league, the Hitters and Missers, which detractors incorrectly predicted would put him out of business. In the '90s, despite fears and misconceptions about AIDS, Morris similarly stood firm in supporting the alley's all-gay league over the protests of some patrons.

Morris expanded to five locations, two of which were sold. In 2006 the name was changed to Pin Chasers. Today Anthony Perrone, the stepson of Morris, is the CEO of the business and can add "global pandemic" to the long list of challenges the family-run business has overcome.

Prior to the transformation of Sparkman's Wharf in Channelside, the world's largest bowling pin stood outside of the bowling alley Splitsville.

1959

Oldest Theme Park

Busch Gardens

10165 McKinley Dr., Tampa

As explained previously, untangling and defining roadside attractions, amusements parks, and theme parks from one another can be complicated. Suffice it to say that theme parks are essentially amusement parks organized around a central concept or theme. Cypress Gardens, established in 1936, likely qualifies as the area's first theme park (the theme being a combination of gardens, southern belles, and watersports), but it was acquired in 2010 and transformed into Legoland Florida.

For longevity, Busch Gardens emerges victorious. The 335-acre African-themed park was originally launched by Anheuser-Busch as a marketing ploy with the name and theme of "The Dark Continent." Along with free admission (and beer) it featured a bird garden and tours of its brewery via the "Stairway to the Stars" escalator. In 1964 August A. Busch Jr. established the popular Old Swiss House restaurant, allegedly as a Valentine's Day gift for his third wife, Trudy. The following year he added the 70-acre Serengeti Plains exhibit, which became the country's largest free-roaming habitat for African animals outside of their home continent.

The '70s saw the beginning of thrill rides and roller-coasters at the park and the end of free admission. The newest of these (technically a reboot of an older ride) is the wood and metal hybrid roller-coaster Iron Gwazi, which joins Tigris, Cheetah

Aerial view of the Anheuser-Busch plant and Busch Gardens taken September 26, 1959. Burgert Brothers photo, courtesy of the Tampa-Hillsborough County Public Library System.

Hunt, the dive coaster SheiKra, and others. In addition to the animal park and rides, Busch Gardens hosts a long-running concert series at its outdoor amphitheater, and the park gets seasonal makeovers for Howl-O-Scream and Christmas Town. Prior to COVID-19, the park had a steady annual attendance of over four million.

Following Anheuser-Busch's acquisition by InBev, it divested its entertainment holdings, including Busch Gardens. The park is now owned and operated by SeaWorld Entertainment, Inc.

In a nod to history, the Legoland park continues the longstanding Cypress Gardens tradition of waterskiing performances, which are now conducted under Brickbeard's LEGO pirate flag.

1961

Oldest State Historical Marker

Tampa Bay Hotel

401 W. Kennedy Blvd., Tampa

It stands to reason that as Florida grows and changes and accrues more history, recording and preserving that history becomes more pressing. Towards that end, in 1960 (six years before the National Register of Historic Places was created) the state established its historical marker program, which today is part of the Florida Division of Historical Resources based in the state capital, Tallahassee. As of 2022, that program has planted roughly 1,200 markers throughout the state recognizing places, peoples, and events that are a minimum of 30 years old.

According to Program Director Michael Hart, the first of these markers planted in the Tampa Bay Area was put in place in 1961 outside of what was once the Tampa Bay Hotel. A reasonable choice, given that the opening of

The Florida State Historical Marker outside of what was once the Tampa Bay Hotel. Photo by the author.

the hotel in 1891 is seen as one of the critical moments in Tampa's transition from small town to major city. The marker recounts how the hotel was erected at a cost of $3 million and connected to Plant's railroad line. The 511-room, Moorish Revival style hotel itself occupied six of the 150 acres along with 20 other buildings, a bowling alley, race track, casino, and heated indoor pool. It featured the state's first elevator as well as electric lights and telephones in each room.

The reverse side of the marker highlights the hotel's role as the headquarters for the invasion of Cuba during the Spanish American War. Among those stationed in the area was one Colonel Theodore "Teddy" Roosevelt, who would lead the conflict's most famous fighting unit, the volunteer cavalry known as the "Rough Riders." That fame was achieved at a hefty price; it had the highest casualty rate of all regiments involved in actions in Cuba.

The hotel became the home of the University of Tampa in 1933 and also houses the Henry B. Plant Museum. It was added to the National Register of Historic Places in 1972 and designated a national historic landmark in 1976.

According to the Historical Marker Database, there are combined more than 500 historical markers and war memorials in Hillsborough, Pinellas, and Manatee Counties.

1967

Oldest Enclosed Shopping Center

WestShore Plaza

250 Westshore Plaza, Tampa

In 1954 Victor Gruen is credited with having built the first modern shopping mall in Edina, Minnesota. Just six years later there were approximately 4,500 of them nationwide. The first of these fully enclosed shopping centers in the Tampa Bay Area was West Shore Plaza Shopping City (now known as WestShore Plaza).

Built on a 50-acre plot, Sumner & Schein designed the structure out of Boston and encompassed roughly 623,400 square feet of fully air-conditioned space, which was a significant differentiator at the time. Anchoring the shopping center was locally based department store Maas Brothers, which occupied three levels and 238,000 square feet. Maas Brothers opened there on October 19, 1966, a year before the rest of the mall. J. C. Penney (the last of the mall's original tenants) welcomed its first shoppers in September of 1967. Other stores at the time included Walgreens, Woolworth's, and a Pantry Pride grocery store.

As other malls opened nearby, WestShore's first expansion in 1974 added a northeast wing, parking garage, and Robinson's as a third anchor. In 1990 following the mall's acquisition by the Grosvenor Group, it was remodeled in the Mediterranean style, which typifies much of the Tampa Bay area's architecture. A third expansion at the west end of the mall coincided with the arrival

(Left) Sunlight spills into the quiet interior of Westshore plaza. (Right) Exterior entrance to the plaza. Photos by the author.

of Saks Fifth Avenue in November of 1998, but the retailer's stay lasted just five years, with Dick's Sporting Goods taking over the space in 2014.

Other retailers have come and gone as well: Maas Brothers became Burdines in 1991, which in turn became Macy's in 2005. Robinson's became Maison Blanche in 1987, which changed to Dillard's in 1991, which became a Sears in 2002 and ultimately closed in March of 2019.

The overall environment for large shopping malls has also faced changes, two of the largest being the rise of internet shopping and more recently, the COVID-19 global pandemic. Today there are an estimated 1,000 malls in the country, less than a quarter of the number when WestShore was first built. Despite the changing shopping mall landscape, the area's oldest endures.

Given the climate of the Tampa Bay area, shopping outdoors is at least as popular as shopping indoors with fairs, farmers markets, and fine art and craft shows in virtually every neighborhood.

1973

Oldest Skyscraper

Park Tower

400 N. Tampa St., Tampa

Just as there is no single official definition of "high-rise," there is no universal agreement as to what constitutes a skyscraper, save that it is a very tall high-rise, which isn't particularly helpful for reasons previously stated. Assuming a minimum height of 100 meters (just over 328 feet), the oldest skyscraper in Tampa to meet this definition would be Park Tower.

Completed in November of 1973, the building rises 36 stories to a height of 140 meters (458 feet). When it was first erected it was the tallest building in the state until it was surpassed in 1981 by One Tampa City Center. Today it holds on to its spot as the sixth-tallest tower in the city and occupies an enviable location across from the Tampa Riverwalk.

Park Tower looks considerably more modern today than it does in this Department of Commerce photograph from February of 1982. Photo courtesy of the State Archives of Florida, Florida Memory.

Initially the tower served as the headquarters for the First National Bank of Tampa and later First National Bank of Florida. It also housed the offices of the Lykes Brothers Corporation (it was known for a time as the Lykes Building). More recently it became the Tampa home of BB&T (formerly Colonial Bank), whose logo adorns the top of the tower. BB&T, however, closed their offices there in January of 2021 following their merger with SunTrust to become Truist, and consolidated their workspace into their newer tower.

The building was purchased in 2006 by Sterling American Property of New York, which oversaw a restoration that included the HVAC and electrical systems. Ten years later the building changed hands and is currently owned by a joint venture between City Office REIT, Tower Realty Partners, and Feldman Equities LLC. In 2019, architecture firm Gensler was selected to modernize the building's facade with a modern lobby, a Buddy Brew Coffee café, and a lighter color for the exterior.

Lykes Insurance is still an anchor tenant there, along with Level 3 Communications and the United States Attorney's office. Also located there beneath the building is a Federal Reserve Vault. The building is both EPA Energy Star and LEED EB Gold Certified.

The first and oldest building in St. Petersburg to meet the 100-meter mark is the residential building Bayfront Plaza, which was built in 1975.

1981

Oldest Thai Buddhist Temple

Wat Mongkolratanaram (Wat Tampa)

5306 Palm River Rd., Tampa

While the Tampa Bay area has long been home to diverse cultures and religious practices, it has become even more so over time. By the 1980s there was a sufficient Thai Buddhist population to warrant creation of the state's first temple. In 1981 Phramongkolthep Moli an assistant abbot from a different temple met with Buddhists from various cities in Florida. They agreed that Tampa should be the location of the temple, given its location near the center of the state. Wat Mongkolratanaram Thai Buddhist Temple was thus established on May 19, 1981, with the vision of providing a place of worship and establishing a school of meditation, a Thai and Asian Cultural Center, a Thai language school, an international religious center, and a point of contact between Thais living abroad and Thai government officials.

In 1983 the ornate temple (an example of Ayudhaya architecture), which was sponsored by the King of Thailand, was moved to its current location along the Palm River. At the time it was home to two monks. In 1990 the adjacent land was acquired, which roughly doubled the size of the temple grounds. This allowed for growth and a new temple and monks quarters, which were dedicated in 2007. A sea wall and benches were also added in 2011.

Located along the Palm River, Wat Tampa draws those seeking to nourish both the spirit and the body. Photo by the author.

Outside of the Thai Buddhist community, Wat Tampa has become popular with residents of all denominations for its Sunday market, which started out with two tables in 1988 and now draws a crowd that packs the parking lot to overflowing. Money from the weekly market and donations support the temple's activities, but the COVID-19 pandemic disrupted this long-running source of income. Volunteers devised a clever solution in the form of a drive-through service to keep the market going. The temple website displays a menu of available drive-through options, as well as a commitment to social distancing, temperature checks, and other safety measures. It also invites visitors to overcome fear and find a sense of calm through meditation, which has quite possibly never been a more prescient and compelling offer.

Sarasota's World Peace Buddhist Temple was opened in 2011 and designed on the celestial palace of Heruka, following the stages along the path to spiritual enlightenment.

1983*

Oldest Hindu Temple

Hindu Temple of Florida

5509 Lynn Rd., Tampa

Originating more than 4,000 years ago, many scholars consider Hinduism to be the world's oldest religion in practice today. It is followed by some 900 million individuals world-wide, including 30,000 or more in the Tampa Bay area (which has Florida's third-largest Indian American population behind Orlando and South Florida). In spite of such a large community, it wasn't until the 1980s that the area's first Hindu temple was established.

Prior to the creation of the Hindu Temple of Florida in December of 1983, observance of Sanātana Dharma, ("Eternal Dharma" as Hinduism is known to its practitioners) occurred mostly in the homes of smaller groups. By 1989 the organization had raised enough funds to purchase 15 acres of land roughly 10 miles north of the Tampa International

The Hindu Temple of Florida as of August 2013. Photo uploaded to Wikipedia by proshob, licensed under CC BY-SA 3.0

Airport. A small building on the property served as a temporary place of worship until construction of the current temple began in 1994.

The initial plan for the temple included an 84-foot-tall Raja gopuram (main tower), but that was lowered slightly to accommodate the runway needs of the airport. At 70 feet tall, it was still the tallest Hindu temple in the United States as of 2021.

In 1996 the sanctification ritual known as Maha Kumbabhishekam was performed, and in 2000 a team of 15 artisans from Southern India began the "Indianization" process, which entailed hand-carving hundreds of elaborate figures and images from Vedic literature and the Hindu pantheon covering the entirety of the Temple's exterior walls. The result is a stunning and unique building, unlike any other in the Tampa Bay area.

Today the temple serves as the spiritual heart of the area's Hindu community. In addition to services conducted by the priests there, it also hosts weddings, birthdays, and other life events. It is also open to the public for education and tours.

**The year 1983 refers to the formation of the 501(c)3 organization rather than to the construction of the temple.*

Those who plan to visit are advised to wear modest clothing and remove their footwear before entering.

1983

Oldest Comic Book Shop

Green Shift Music and Comics

5713 N. Nebraska Ave., Tampa

The first time Don Taylor met Peter Parker, Taylor was about nine years old, and Parker had been a high school student for decades. Of course they didn't meet in person, but rather in the pages of one of the two comic books Taylor bought each week with his 25-cent allowance. By the time Taylor graduated high school he was an avid collector, an activity he returned to after college and meeting his wife.

The dawn of the 1980s found mild-mannered Taylor working nights at a hotel and days at a music store named Green Shift. Shortly thereafter, the owner sold the store to one of Taylor's friends, who ran it briefly as a pawn shop. When that ended in 1983, Taylor bought the store, which he planned to continue as a music store. When he moved his comic book collection from his grandmother's home to the extra room at Green Shift, he quickly discovered that people were more interested in learning about Gotham's Dark Knight than in practicing chord progressions. So a comic book store it became.

The gambit paid off and by 1987 Taylor had moved to a bigger location at 5226 North Nebraska. Taylor remembers the 1990s as the heyday for comic books, when plotlines became more complex and the big publishers were joined by a wave of smaller independents like Dark Horse and Image. For a time, he even had a second store to keep up with demand.

Green Shift harkens back to a time when collectors examined the spines of comic books to differentiate "very fine" from "near mint." Photo courtesy of Green Shift Music and Comics.

Today from the store's current location, things look a bit different—Miles Morales now wears the webslinger's costume and Disney's purchase of Marvel has made comic book stories known the world over. According to Taylor, the accessibility of the content on the internet, the big screen, and streaming services are actually diminishing interest in their original paper format. COVID-19 also hit the business hard, taking the lives of at least two of Taylor's longtime regular customers. He can imagine a not-too-distant future when comic books will exist only in digital format.

Until that day comes, for the true believers there is still Green Shift.

Green Shift is a reference to how wooden instruments are made, not to the color of a superhero's lantern or to Dr. Bruce Banner becoming the hulk.

1992

OLDEST ALL-FEMALE GASPARILLA PIRATE KREWE

YE LOYAL KREWE OF GRACE O'MALLEY

It would be difficult (and frankly less fun) to try telling the story of the Tampa Bay area without a chapter on pirates. Although the area's most celebrated pirate, Jose Gaspar (or Gasparilla), was probably fictional, the Gulf of Mexico was once prowled by very real pirates such as Diego "El Mulato" Martin from Cuba.

A fact that may surprise some about piracy is how diverse and inclusive a trade it was. Crews were often composed of a plethora of nationalities and ethnicities, including former slaves who were sometimes given the choice of perishing with their captors or serving as free men and pirate crewmembers entitled to their fair share of plunder. Such may have been the true origin story of the pirate (or pirates) known as "Black Caesar," who served aboard Blackbeard's flagship, *Queen Anne's Revenge*.

The profession was also open to all genders, with numerous notable female pirates including the Chinese Cheng I Sao, Anne Bonny and Mary Reed (both of whom were Calico Jack Rackham's crewmates), and the Irish "Pirate Queen" Grace O'Malley.

Despite women having proven for centuries that they were every bit as capable pirates as men, and despite the Gasparilla festival owing its existence since 1904 in large part to Miss Louise Francis Dodge (who was the *Tampa Bay Tribune*'s society editor),

This creatively assembled collection of pins, coins, and other objects related to Ye Loyal Krewe of Grace O'Malley is preserved at the Tampa Bay History Center. Photo by the author.

it wasn't until the 1990s that the first all-female pirate Krewe joined in the festivities as Ye Loyal Krewe of Grace O'Malley (a.k.a. "Ladies of Grace").

Founded by 14 women, the organization has since grown to include over 250 members who participate in more than a half-dozen annual parades, not only including Gasparilla but also the Sant' Yago Knight Parade, the Rough Riders St. Patrick's Day Parade, and Springtime Tallahassee. They adopted as their motto "fun, friendship, and frivolity" and the seahorse as their mascot—of which a giant moving version adorns the float they constructed in 2007. Invitations to become a full, cutlass-carrying member of the group are nearly as coveted as gold doubloons and made available from time to time via lottery system to those who have previously volunteered.

Legends persist of hidden pirate treasures throughout Florida. Along the Gulf Coast, some believe that Billy Bowlegs Rogers stashed his ill-gotten gains near Santa Rosa Island.

1993

Oldest Skatepark

Skatepark of Tampa (SPoT)

4215 E. Columbus Dr., Tampa

Skateboarding was invented in the 1950s and as the sport gained traction, dedicated skateparks emerged beginning with Surf City in Tucson, Arizona, in 1965. Surf City is long gone now, making Kona Skatepark in Jacksonville, Florida, (built in 1977) now the oldest operating skatepark on earth per the *Guinness Book of World Records*.

Tampa was also home to one of sport's most iconic parks, the Perry Harvey Sr. Park Skateboard Bowl (better known as the "Bro Bowl"), which opened in 1979. While most skateparks at the time charged a fee, the Bro Bowl was free to the public. Before being

Images from the early days of SPoT, courtesy of Paul Zitzer.

demolished in 2015, it was featured in videos and documentaries, and even carved out an enduring place in history as the first skatepark ever added to the National Register of Historic Places.

Brian Schaefer created Skatepark of Tampa (SPoT) in 1993 when he and his friends needed a new place to skate after an angry homeless mob attempted to burn down their former hangout. The warehouse they moved to has since become legendary. Plenty of skateboarding icons have competed in Tampa Pro and Tampa Am events there including Mike Vallely, Danny Way, and Tony Hawk, who featured SPoT's terrain-style main course (currently being rebuilt) in the video games *Tony Hawk's Underground* and *Tony Hawk's Pro Skater 2x*.

SPoT has evolved to include a retail area with boards, footwear, and apparel; an outdoor bowl and a kiddie-course; a snack bar; art gallery; and the Transitions music venue. From time-to-time music and entertainment celebrities have been known to drop in like comedian Dave Chappelle, who had an after-hours session there for his friends in 2004, and since 2011, Lil Wayne has been a regular attendee at the Tampa Pro contests.

Now 29 years old, SPoT is well on its way towards its goal of "'93 to infinity."

For those who prefer snowboarding to skateboarding, the area's first and only snow park, Snowcat Ridge, is now open in Dade City

---

1994

Oldest Tattoo Parlor

Blue Devil Tattoo

1603 E. 7th Ave., Tampa

Artwork in the Tampa Bay area has extended beyond museums and galleries to cover virtually every available surface, from exterior building walls (especially during St. Petersburg's annual SHINE Mural Festival) to the human body itself. But the art of tattooing was maligned for far longer than it's been embraced.

The first wave of tattoos to arrive in the US were those worn by sailors returning from World War I, inked with designs from distant shores where they were stationed. It was later adopted as a practice by motorcycle clubs, but drunken sailors and bikers weren't exactly the types of characters that Tampa was eager to embrace. Instead, the city joined New York and others in banning tattoo parlors, which lasted until 1994 (one exception being Lou's Tattoos, which held the title of "Oldest Tattoo Parlor in Florida" until it closed permanently during the COVID-19 pandemic).

Following the city's change of position, Annette LaRue became the first Ybor City applicant to receive a license for a tattoo parlor. There among the cafes and old cigar shops Blue Devil added new color to the neighborhood. It was voted "Best in Tampa Bay" for the next six consecutive years, by which time it had solidified a reputation for quality and artistry among the nascent and tightly knit community. Current owner Rob Feierstadt remembers being part of those early days. "Instead of going out to the clubs, we hung out there at the shop and shared our ideas and artwork."

Today Blue Devil operates in its original location in Ybor City. Photos by the author.

Since taking over for LaRue in 2000, Feierstadt has maintained Blue Devil's atmosphere, which was legendary locally long before the shop appeared in documentaries and the film *Magic Mike*.

Today tattoos are as much a part of the local culture as Cuban sandwiches, which keeps Blue Devil's staff of five tattoo and piercing artists busy. Some artists have come and gone, often on the way to starting their own shops, but Feierstadt doesn't see them as competitors as much as extended family. He can look with pride at what his shop helped create, knowing that the impression it has left on Tampa is truly indelible.

Other iconic Ybor City tattoo shops include Atomic Tattoos, Ybor City Tattoo Company, and Las Vegas Tattoo Co. Tampa's annual tattoo convention also brings big artists and crowds to town.

2002

Oldest Hillsborough County Dog Parks

West Park Dog Park and Mango Dog Park

6402 N. Occident St., Tampa, and 11717 Clay Pit Rd., Seffner

Berkley California in the 1960s and 1970s was a central point for America's counterculture, unleashing a bevy of revolutionary new ideas throughout the country that included the free speech movement, Vietnam War protests, experimentation with psychedelic drugs . . . and dog parks. While that last one may have escaped the attention of many historians, it has proven no less enduring than any of the other concepts produced at that time and place.

In 1979 the Experimental Dog Park in Ohlone Park was established by Martha Scott Benedict and Doris Richards. Since then, the park's success has led to the creation of as many as 2,000 similarly styled dog parks through the nation, but the trend would have to sit and wait patiently for another 23 years before Hillsborough County adopted it.

In 1999 residents approached the county's parks and recreation department about the idea. The department was likely already chewing on the idea, which may have come to their attention through a national parks and recreation newsletter that had begun circulating. Parks and recreation manager and pet owner Lois Kessler decided to explore the matter further with a trip north to see what dog parks in other cities and states looked like.

Tinker Bell the shih tzu examines some of the hoops and other features at the West Park Dog Park. Photo by the author.

Upon returning to Tampa, it was determined that not one, but two dog parks should be built simultaneously: one in the north connected to the West Park Sports Complex and another in the south-east within Mango park. By 2001 the projects were funded, and in 2002 they opened to the public. A part-time recreation leader was assigned to both parks to keep them clean, gather feedback, and coordinate events like canine costume contests.

Both dog parks include a five-acre play area surrounded by a six-foot chain-link fence with separate areas for large and small dogs, along with a dog washing station, human and dog water fountains, shelters, and picnic tables. Based on its popularity, the Mango Dog Park underwent a major renovation in 2020, nearly doubling its size. The West Park Dog Park is equally well loved, with a respectable rating of four and a half bones on the BringFido website.

Dogs in the Tampa Bay area don't just get to go to the park, they can also enjoy the beach. Fort De Soto Dog Beach consistently ranks as a local favorite.

2005

Oldest Alligator Attraction

Croc Encounters

8703 Bowles Rd., Tampa

Since long before Florida became the 27th US state, before the first Europeans came searching for riches, before even the area's first indigenous people arrived, there have been gators (and, to a lesser extent, crocodiles). These predatory reptiles (known collectively as crocodilians) have become perhaps the single most ubiquitous symbol of the Sunshine State. Some may be old enough to have brought them home from vacations as pets (until they outgrew bathtubs and tanks) or recall visiting attractions like Orlando's Gatorland. While gators and crocs can be found in virtually every zoo, aquarium, and even some miniature golf courses throughout the state, the oldest place in Tampa where they play the starring role wasn't hatched until 2005.

"Jungle John" Paner was working with animals and by 1999 his focus had become crocodilians. This coincided with the arrival in his life of Amos, an out-of-state alligator who had outgrown the tank he lived in. John and his wife, "Krocodile Karina" Sura Paner, took in the wayward reptile and became licensed to utilize him for educational purposes. This led to more requests from individuals seeking to rehome a variety of animals.

By February of 2005 the couple had acquired land in the Temple Terrace neighborhood, where they set up operations to

Amos and his crocodilian companions spend their time lounging when they're not educating the public. Photos courtesy of Croc Encounters.

accommodate more than 300 animals. They have also added their two sons, "Jungle Johnny" and "Jungle Jake," to their roster.

During COVID-19, Croc Encounters went into a deep hibernation and has since awakened to new challenges including recovering from lost revenue and facing increased expenses on everything from lumber for repairs to feed for the animals. They are pulling a page out of the ancient playbook held by their own crocodilians as they adapt and scale their business.

As for Amos, he's still with them today. He's a bit larger than when he first joined the family, now measuring 13 feet and over 800 pounds, and spends most of his time happily basking in the sun.

Anyone seeking to get really close to a gator can take the Alligator & Wildlife Discovery Center at Madeira Beach up on the offer to "kiss a gator."

2015

Oldest Gold Star Family Memorial Monument

Monument on the Front Lawn of Franklin Middle Magnet School

3915 E. 21st Ave., Tampa

Since its inception, the story of Tampa and that of the military have been inexorably bound. All that the city has become essentially sprang from Fort Brooke, which was established in 1824 under Florida's first territorial governor, Andrew Jackson. The area's military tradition has continued through the Seminole Wars, the Civil War, as the point from which troops were sent to Cuba during the Spanish-American War, and up through America's most recent wars in Iraq and Afghanistan. Hotels like the Don Cesar and the Tampa Bay Hotel as well as Drew Field, Rocky Point Golf Course, and other locations have all been used by armed forces as some point. Tampa is also home to MacDill Airforce Base and, since 1983, the United States Central Command (CENTCOM).

Having so many service members stationed in Tampa means inevitably that some have made the ultimate sacrifice. The families they leave behind are known as "Gold Star Families," which traces back to the practice in World War I of military families displaying flags with a blue star for each immediate family member serving in the armed forces. When one of those service members lost his/her lives in the war, their blue star was changed to gold.

The design of the memorial makes powerful use of negative space. Photo by the author.

Hershel "Woody" Williams came to know many such families. After displaying "valiant devotion to duty" as a marine at the Battle of Iwo Jima in World War II, he was awarded the Congressional Medal of Honor. He then founded his own organization which, among its other endeavors, has been establishing Gold Star Family Memorial Monuments throughout the country. The first of these monuments erected in Florida was placed on the front lawn of Franklin Middle Magnet School on May 21, 2015. On one side of the monument is inscribed "Gold Star Families Memorial Monument, a tribute to Gold Star Families and Relatives who sacrificed a Loved One for our Freedom," and on the other side four panels depict Homeland, Family, Patriot, and Sacrifice. To date, 91 such monuments have been installed in 50 states and one US Territory.

According to the Tampa Bay Economic Development Council, more than 100,000 veterans live and work in the Tampa Bay area.

PINELLAS COUNTY

~900 CE

Oldest Preserved Open-Water Wooden Canoe

Prehistoric Canoe at Weedon Island Preserve

1800 Weedon Dr. NE, St. Petersburg, FL 33702

From time to time, natural processes such as erosion and the churning of large bodies of water by intense storms will reveal various trinkets and treasures dating back to when Florida was in the hands of the Spaniards. Every once in a rare while, even older artifacts are exposed, such as tools and materials from the area's indigenous cultures.

Such was the case in 2001 when St. Petersburg resident Harry Koran happened to notice something long and straight embedded the sand near Weedon Island Preserve. He began digging around what looked like a felled tree, felt the inner curve of it, and wondered if it was of archaeological significance. He connected shortly thereafter with Phyllis E. Kolianos, the environmental-education coordinator for the Weedon Island Preserve Cultural and Natural History Center, who helped coordinate an investigation into Koran's find.

A team of experts confirmed what Koran suspected: that he had discovered something very special indeed. Measuring just under forty feet from its bow to broken stern, the team identified it as the first and oldest open-water dugout canoe found in Florida (more recently, others have been found as well, though none of the same length). Subsequent testing and carbon dating

The preserved portion of the canoe is now publicly displayed. Photos by the author with permission from the Weedon Island Preserve Cultural and Natural History Center.

determined that the vessel was made of pine and around 1,100 years old. Accounts from Spanish explorers to the area had described such vessels, and analysis of artifacts also suggested the existence of open-water vessels, but the discovery at Weedon Island provided hard evidence.

After years of being carefully bathed in preservation tanks, cleaned, and conserved, the canoe is now on display at the Weedon Island Preserve Cultural and Natural History Center.

Weedon Island is a Pinellas County treasure—its 3,190 acres are home to upland and aquatic ecosystems teeming with native flora and fauna.

1852

Oldest Preserved Two-Story Family Home

The McMullen-Coachman Log Cabin

11909 125th St., Largo, FL 33774

As was the case with many of the figures who played a role in the development of the Tampa Bay area, it was health reasons that first brought James P. McMullen to what is present-day Pinellas County. At the age of 18, following a diagnosis of consumption (tuberculosis), he left his family in Georgia to recuperate in the area known today as Rocky Point. Even though he rejoined his family to the north, he would return to settle near Tampa Bay twice more, once in 1848 where he and his wife faced insurmountable challenges in the form of both hostile Native Americans and the devastating "Gale of '48," before successfully settling there around 1850.

It was here that he built a four-room log cabin with a second floor, which was an uncommon feature among pioneer dwellings at the time. It was built of resilient heart pine, which would all

The McMullen-Coachman Log Cabin at its current location inside Heritage Village. Photo by the author.

but vanish as the area was further settled. The cabin was designed with a central breezeway and intentional gaps for air circulation, which was especially significant for those like James with health issues.

The McMullen home became a meeting place for locals as well as a beacon to other McMullen family members. James's younger brother, Daniel, moved to the area to the area in 1852 (homesteading in present-day Largo) and joined his sibling in the cattle business. A third brother, John Fain, followed shortly thereafter. Eventually, a total of seven McMullen brothers and their families would make their way to the area and play their part in transforming the wilderness into Clearwater and other towns of central Pinellas County, building schools, cultivating the land, and getting involved in local politics.

The cabin James built continued to serve the McMullen Family until the land and the cabin were acquired in 1901 by the Coachman Family. In the 1930s, the Coachmans opened the structure to the public. By the 1960s, it was primarily being used for storage. It suffered arson damage in 1976. The following year, it was relocated to Heritage Village in Largo, where it was restored and once again opened to the public, complete with era-appropriate, handmade furnishings.

Heritage Village has many historical buildings and points of interest including the Harris School Building, the House of Seven Gables, the Turner Bungalow, and the H. C. Smith Store.

1895

OLDEST PUBLIC LIBRARY

DUNEDIN PUBLIC LIBRARY

223 Douglas Ave., Dunedin, FL 34698

Of the many invasive species that have made a home for themselves in the Tampa Bay area, few are capable of generating as much ire from locals as the seasonal, migratory "snow birds,"—vacationers who come to escape the harsh northern winters. According to a social media study conducted in 2019, Tampa complains more about the presence of these visitors than any other city in the United States. While it's true that they contribute to increased traffic and car accidents, it's also true that at least occasionally their contributions are of great benefit.

Such is the case with Pinellas County's oldest library. Christopher B. Bouton was a winter resident of the area from Cleveland, Ohio, who decided to donate 200 books from his personal library to the city of Dunedin "for public use." Bouton's generosity, however, required that the city have a place to keep his gift. It so happened that Bouton's brother owned the local meeting hall (situated on the waterfront of what is now Edgewater Park), which he transferred to Dunedin Library Association. Here the initial 200 volumes grew to 7,000 and by the time the city took ownership of the library in 1935, it had outgrown its birthplace.

A new library was built in 1956 on Louden Avenue (a second library was also erected on Main Street in 1964, which is now Dunedin City Hall). The Dunedin Friends of the Library were

Today the library has a more permanent home next door to TD Ballpark where a different set of migratory birds—the Toronto Blue Jays come to train each spring.

established in 1962 and continue to provide support. In 1976 the library moved again to a space in the Douglas Plaza Shopping Center, which more than quadrupled its size to over 20,000 square feet.

In April of 1995, just after the library celebrated its centennial, the books were moved to storage so that the old building could be demolished and a new library built on the same site by Harvard Jolly Architects. The new facility had been made possible when, six years earlier, retired attorney Franklin Chase Milliken left his estate to the city to benefit the library. Today, the library continues to evolve, integrating new technology, and proving that snow birds aren't all bad.

Within Hillsborough County, the oldest operating library is the West Tampa Branch Library, which was established with a Carnegie grant in 1914.

1897

Oldest Hotel

The Belleview Inn (Formerly a portion of the Hotel Belleview)

25 Belleview Blvd., Belleair, FL 33756

Of railroad magnate Henry B. Plant's eight hotels, the best known—with its iconic cupolas—is undoubtedly his beloved Tampa Bay Hotel. The only one of his hotels which continues to operate today, however, is part of the Tampa Bay Hotel's younger sister, the Belleview Inn.

While less opulent than the Tampa Bay Hotel, it was still a thing of beauty when the Hotel Belleview opened in 1897. With electric lights in each of the 145 guest rooms, a telegraph in the lobby, and ornate peaked gables, by World War II (after Henry Flagler's larger hotels had been demolished) it was the largest wooden structure in the state. It was also the last of Henry Plant's hotels—he died just two years later. When his son, Morton Plant,

(Left) The White Queen has today been restored as the Belleview Inn. Photo by the author. (Right) This 1922 Burgert Brothers photo shows the massive original Belleview Hotel. Photo courtesy of the Tampa-Hillsborough County Public Library System.

took over the hotel he painted it white with green roof tiles, after which it was known as the "White Queen on the Gulf."

In the 1920s the hotel thrived under John McEntee Bowman ownership and under a new name, the Belleview-Biltmore. Famous visitors at the time included the Duke of Windsor, the DuPonts, Thomas Edison, Henry Ford, Babe Ruth, and Joe DiMaggio.

World War II put the hotel to use as lodging for servicemen stationed nearby. After the war, the hotel was acquired by Bernard F. Powell. In 1979 it was added to the US Register of Historic Places and continued to host big names including Bob Dylan, Margaret Thatcher, and presidents Ford, Carter, Bush, and Obama.

By the 1980s the hotel was in decline. It changed hands multiple times, first to the Japanese-based Mido Development in the early 1990s and then to hotelier Salim Jetha in 1997. Despite various attempts to save the hotel, it closed in 2009 and JMC Communities began demolition in 2015 to make way for condominiums. In 2017 it was removed from the National Register.

But the White Queen wasn't ready to abdicate her throne just yet. The last remaining portion (about 10 percent) of the original structure was relocated to a new foundation at its present location, restored and reopened as the boutique Belleview Inn. Today the hotel is a member of Historic Hotels of America.

Henry B. Plant left his mark on the Tampa Bay area with more than railroads and hotels—the city's seal is a depiction of his steamship, Mascotte.

1911

Oldest Incorporated Beach Community in Pinellas County

Pass-a-Grille

If determining the area's earliest beach communities seems like it should be a simple matter, consider this—for thousands of years, indigenous people made temporary and permanent settlements along the coastline. Later, European and then American settlers similarly set up their own fishing camps and shelters on what today are many of the area's most popular beaches. But going to the beach, which now constitutes one of the area's most popular activities, wasn't something people typically did for pleasure until the early 20th century. A far cry from the stunning, white sand beaches that have drawn tourists the world over, the area's early beaches were mostly overgrown, mosquito-infested saltmarshes, seldom visited for purposes other than cartography, scientific inquiry, or on doctor's orders.

When Zephaniah Phillips became Pass-a-Grille's first permanent resident there after the Civil War, he couldn't possibly have imagined that the costal wilderness in which he homesteaded would one day be so popular that parking would be in short supply. In 1892, he sold a portion of his property to Dr. Gehring, who planned to build a hotel and sanitarium like that which would come to be in Safety Harbor, but ended up selling to

1941 aerial view of Pass-A-Grille military barracks. Photo courtesy of the Pinellas Public Library Cooperative, Pinellas Memory Digital Collection.

other developers. By the turn of the century there were a half-dozen houses. In 1902, Joseph E. Merry opened the town's first general store (and post office) on his eponymously named pier. La Plaza was opened shortly thereafter and more homes were built as Pass-a-Grille started to become a destination for visitors. By 1912 the community had five hotels but still relatively few permanent residents.

Pass-a-Grille became the first of the towns in the Gulf Beaches to officially incorporate in 1911, by which time a boat connected to the trolly systems was already providing transportation. The McAdoo Bridge opened in 1919, the Gandy Bridge three years later, and in 1928, the famous pink Don CeSar Palace opened its doors. Since then, Pass-a-Grille has weathered fires, hurricanes, and economic depressions. In 1989, it was designated a US Historic District and has a total estimated population today north of 16,000.

The name "Pass-a-Grille" is thought to be either a mangled version of the French name, "Passe aux Grilleurs," or a reference to early fishermen there at "Pass to the Grillers."

1912

Oldest Family-Owned Shoe Repair Shop

Faklis' Department Store & Shoe Repair

139 E. Tarpon Ave., Tarpon Springs, FL 34689

Tarpon Springs today is best known for its sponge diving industry, which was the vision of John Cheney, who established the Cheney Sponge Company. By 1905, his company employed over 500 sponge divers who came largely from the Dodecanese Islands and other parts of Greece. With that large of a local business, others were quick to realize that the growing community would have other needs, too. To meet that demand, Tarapani's Department Store opened in 1911 and just a year later, Faklis' Department Store & Shoe Repair followed suit across the street.

Vasile George Faklis was born in Greece in 1892 and learned the shoe repair business from an uncle, after which he and his brother apprenticed at a shoe factory in Symi. He moved to north Pinellas County when it was still part of Hillsborough County, served in World War I, and returned to grow his business and raise a family. He started out making new shoes, but had to adapt during the Great Depression, which meant repairing rather than manufacturing shoes. He passed on his business and repair skills to his sons, George and Michael, who in turn passed the torch to the founder's grandson and current owner, also named Vasile George Faklis.

(Left) Photo of the original 1912-era equipment, courtesy of the Faklis family. (Right) The current storefront in Tarpon Springs. Photo by the author.

Over multiple generations, the store has evolved and moved to its current location. For a time, it was a full-service department store with clothes, hats, suits, and other goods, although its present day retail offerings are primarily foot- and shoe-focused. In 1994, Vasile added an orthotic clinic to his grandfather's store with an on-site physical and occupational therapist. He also became the only one statewide to hold German certification in sensorimotor insoles.

Despite those changes, today multiple generations still work side-by-side in the repair shop and behind the counter. Framed on the wall are pictures and articles detailing the store's history, and display cases throughout the space include some of the original equipment and footwear they've serviced, including a heavy sponge diver's boot.

Tarapani's is still in business as well and located directly across the street from Faklis'. It's no longer a department store though; today they deal in antiques, textiles, and artwork.

1916

Oldest Open Air Post Office

Historic Open Air Post Office, St. Petersburg

3135 1st Ave. N., St. Petersburg, FL 33730

Florida's love affair with Mediterranean Revival-style architecture is evident in buildings throughout the state. Several can be found in St. Petersburg and include buildings such as the Vinoy Hotel, The Princess Martha Hotel, St. Mary's Church, and Comfort Station One. This style also extends to a post office located at the corner of 1st Avenue North and 4th Street North.

The post office has been a functional landmark in continuous operation since 1916, when Woodrow Wilson was President of

It's hard today to imagine a time when Mediterranean Revival Style architecture would have been considered out of place anywhere in the Tampa Bay area. Photo by the author.

the United States. In 1975, it was added to the National Register of Historic Places. A plaque affixed to the post office reads: "The Nation's First Open Air Post Office Corner Stone. Laid on October 12, 1916. Completed and Dedicated on September 27, 1917."

According to an article in the local *Green Bench Monthly*, there's more to the story. In 1907, St. Petersburg Postmaster Roy S. Hanna recommended that the facade be left off the post office. It was his belief that this would improve accessibility and allow residents to get their mail any time of day or night.

The federal postal authorities, however, were considerably less than thrilled with the idea. As a demonstration of their unhappiness with the architectural deviation, they refused to pay rent based on the design. Eventually, they relented and resumed rent payments only after a postmasters' convention held a few months later in St. Petersburg. During the event, government officials approved the design as an appropriate adaptation for the needs of the city.

Eventually outgrowing its original open-air location, the post office briefly moved to the first floor of city hall while Congress approved funds for the full-service post office. For more than a century, it has served the city in a style that is uniquely and distinctly Floridian.

Near the rear of the building is a small postal museum, which includes an old leather mailbag, postcards, and a postal money order purchased by St. Petersburg founder John C. Williams.

1922

OLDEST MUSEUM

ST. PETERSBURG MUSEUM OF HISTORY

335 2nd Ave. NE, St. Petersburg, FL 33701

Mary Wheeler Eaton was by all accounts accustomed to getting what she wanted. The owner of one of St. Petersburg's largest citrus groves and a supporter of no less than 30 different civic organizations, when she declared in a speech at City Hall in July of 1920 that it was time the city had an organization to "discover, secure and preserve [. . .] all matters of historical interest," she had the power and persistence to make it happen.

The first step was to charter the Memorial Historical Society on July 27, 1920, with a petition signed by 70 individuals. The society's first home was provided by the city (where the Museum of Fine Art is today), with the agreement that they maintain it; however, they failed to make the required improvements and lost possession of it after a year.

Shortly thereafter, the Hurricane of 1921 (technically a tropical storm by today's standards) carved a path of destruction through Tampa Bay area, the St. Petersburg Pier notwithstanding. But where others saw only devastation, Mary Wheeler Eaton saw opportunity that would give her vision a literal new lease on life. One of the casualties of the storm was R.W. Main's aquarium at the foot of the pier—saltwater had contaminated its tanks and forced it to close. Wheeler Eaton negotiated and completed the purchase of the building for $6,500 in February of 1922 as a

When it first opened, the museum occupied just a small portion of its current structure. Photo courtesy of the St. Petersburg Museum of History.

permanent home for the historical society. It opened its doors that same year as a museum.

By the time Wheeler Eaton passed away from pneumonia in 1929, her nascent organization could claim 170 paying members. Since that time, the museum has gone through multiple expansions, today housing over 30,000 artifacts with a member base of over 500 families and individuals. It is not only the oldest museum in the Tampa Bay area, but also the third-oldest in the state of Florida.

The museum is currently preparing to celebrate its centennial by breaking ground on a 10,000-square-foot, two-story expansion including a rooftop terrace and a state-of-the-art exhibit gallery.

The St. Petersburg Museum is a fascinating place to explore, from its Little Cooperstown to its collection of items that belonged to Tony Jannus, to its odditorium.

1926

Oldest Health Spa

Safety Harbor Resort and Spa

105 N. Bayshore Dr., Safety Harbor, FL 34695

Stories abound regarding Florida's healing waters, many of which flow from the tale of Ponce de Leon's search for the fabled Fountain of Youth (a story, it turns out, that's as much a myth as its subject matter). Regardless of the validity of such fables, Hernando de Soto would have been aware of them when he arrived and explored the area in 1539, at which point he is said to have come upon the five natural mineral springs in what today is the town of Safety Harbor. He named them Espiritu Santo Springs, believing perhaps that he had found the legendary restorative fountain that his well-known predecessor (hadn't) sought.

Though the Spaniards came and went, the waters and their alleged healing properties remained. When Colonel William Bailey took ownership of the land and the springs in 1855, he worked his own magic in transforming local lore into a steady stream of revenue from tourists. Meanwhile, his son-in-

1925 Burgert Brothers photo of the Safety Harbor Sanatorium with Old Tampa Bay in the background. Photo courtesy of the Pinellas Public Library Cooperative, Pinellas Memory Digital Collection.

View of the interior of the resort and spa from the entranceway. Photo by the author.

law expanded both the marketing and amenities to include a pavilion, swimming pool, and water-bottling operation. When James Felix Tucker died in 1913, his wife Virginia continued the business until her own death in 1931. It was under her leadership that the Safety Harbor Sanitorium was constructed, opening its doors to the public in 1926.

In 1945 Dr. Salem H. Baranoff became the owner of the facility and hotel, giving it the title of health spa for the first time and combining the therapeutic waters with body and skin treatments that are still offered to guests. Once again under new ownership, today its amenities include a 50,000 square foot spa and fitness center with 40 treatment rooms and dozens of weekly fitness classes as well as five clay tennis courts. The hotel has 175 rooms as well as the Fountain Grille Restaurant and a Tiki Bar.

In 1964 the Safety Harbor Spa was recognized by the US Department of the Interior as a historical landmark, and in 1997 it became a Florida Heritage Landmark as well.

One of the rooms on the second floor has been preserved so that visitors can get a glimpse into the history of the resort and spa.

1936*

Oldest Roadside Attraction

Sunken Gardens

1825 4th St. N., St. Petersburg, FL 33704

No discussion of the Tampa Bay area could be complete without touching on the subject of roadside attractions, amusement parks, and theme parks, but differentiating them from each other gets tricky (especially since they all share a common ancestor in Silver Springs Park's glass bottom boats, which first launched in 1870). For the sake of this work, amusement parks are defined as those which feature attractions or entertainment, and theme parks are a subgenre organized around a central theme, like the characters of an animation studio.

Then there are the roadside attractions—oddities that don't fit comfortably into the categories previously mentioned. Some, like Weeki Wachee's mermaid shows, were designed to draw a crowd, while others, like artist Howard Solomon's metal castle and Hong Kong Willie's abode, started out serving more practical purposes. Yet others, like Sunken Gardens, sprouted unexpectedly into something that has drawn curiosity seekers now for nearly 120 years.

The story, which is familiar to many, begins when George and Eula Turner purchased 4.1 acres of land in two separate sections (in 1909 and 1911). George then drained the water from a lake on the property to plant a garden. The rich soil there, which was below sea level, proved perfect for his purpose, and from it sprang a veritable jungle, through which he laid winding paths. A stone from the lake was preserved and has become the source of an urban myth, which claims that any who sit upon the "Grow Stone," as it is known, will be granted a magical green thumb.

The garden evolved to include a nursery where the Turners sold fresh fruit and vegetables. When Turner passed on in 1961, his sons continued his legacy, to which they added the self-proclaimed "World's Largest Gift Shop" and the King of Kings Wax Museum, which existed there from 1968 until the 1990s when the figures made a pilgrimage to the Museum of Religious Arts in Logan, Iowa.

In 1999, the City of St. Petersburg acquired the gardens, which include over 50,000 tropical plants and flowers as well as flamingos and other animals. Today, it is a perennially popular spot to catch a gardening demonstration or host an event.

**The garden existed well before this, but the Turners did not consider it an "attraction" until 1936 when it was walled in and they began charging admission.*

Another long-running roadside attraction worth a visit is Sarasota Jungle Gardens, where visitors can witness a bicycle-riding parrot.

1938

Oldest Architecture Firm

Harvard Jolly Architects

2714 Dr M.L.K Jr St. N., St. Petersburg, FL 33704

If it was architects Malachi Leo Elliott and his peers who were responsible for much of the Tampa Bay area's Mediterranean Revival Style through the 1920s, it was William B. Harvard across the bay in St. Petersburg who penned its next chapter in the style he pioneered and termed "Modern Tropical."

Born in Waldo, Florida, Harvard attended the University of Cincinnati before returning to the Sunshine State and establishing his own firm in 1938. One of his first major projects was the expansion of St. Joseph's Hospital, which led to a 60-year relationship and gave him credentials in the healthcare design niche. The following decade, he completed another key project in the Williams Park Band Shell and Pavilion, which further broke

Shown here are two of the firm's most iconic projects: Pasadena Community Church and the St. Petersburg's Municipal Pier. Photos courtesy of Harvard Jolley Architects.

the conventional mold and earned a coveted Test of Time Award from the American Institute of Architects. Harvard ended the 1950s with the design of the Busch Gardens Hospitality House that featured a floating roof and cantilevered balcony over a natural lagoon.

In 1961 the firm added to its name that of Blanchard E. Jolly, who had joined the firm as a junior draftsman and quickly worked his way up to managing partner. Two years later, the firm designed the Pasadena Community Church in St. Petersburg, which is an example of unique and iconic design. Its dramatic "folded roof" design has been called "one of America's most striking examples of contemporary religious architecture." Perhaps their best-known project was completed in 1973—the St.

Petersburg's Municipal Pier with its innovative and memorable inverted pyramid shape.

The firm completed scores of designs and projects including over 120 libraries (for which they have received 19 awards), as well as schools, hospitals, and fine arts projects. Though Harvard passed away in 1995, the firm has maintained its reputation for innovation with projects like the canyon-like design of the James Museum of Western and Wildlife Art, which was the result of a joint venture with Yann Weymouth as the St. Pete Design Group.

Today the architecture firm is both the area's oldest and one of largest in the State of Florida with offices in St. Petersburg as well as Tampa, Orlando, Sarasota, Fort Myers, Jacksonville, and West Palm Beach. They specialize in healthcare, K-12 education, colleges & universities, and civic architecture.

Architecture enthusiasts should also make a point of visiting Hyde Park Village, which has preserved many of its bungalow and craftsman style homes.

1951

OLDEST DINER

THE CHATTAWAY

358 22nd Ave. S., St. Petersburg, FL 33705

Prior to March of 2021, this chapter would have been about St. Petersburg's iconic Coney Island Sandwich Shop, which was opened in 1926 by Greek Immigrant Peter H. Barlas. It closed just shy of its centennial birthday, citing health concerns and labor shortages brought about by the COVID-19 pandemic. There has been occasional chatter and internet scuttlebutt suggesting that the founder's son, Hank, may yet revive it, but until such time, the title of "oldest currently operating" belongs elsewhere, though where isn't so clear cut. A strict interpretation of "diner" as being a casual restaurant serving American cuisine with both booths and a long sit-down counter would probably require either going south to Waffle House in Sarasota (1956) or north to Brooksville's Coney Island Drive-In (1960), both of which, interestingly, once served Elvis Presley.

Assuming one is willing to accept a broader definition of diner as a casual eatery serving fries, burgers, and other fare from the griddle, then the Chattaway, established in 1951 in St. Petersburg, appears to be next in the line of succession.

Although its current iteration dates to 1951, the history of the location goes back as far as the 1920s when it was a gas station and store. Following the repeal of Prohibition in 1933 it became a restaurant and was given the name Chattaway by former owner and circus aerialist Wiley Franks. In 1951 British expatriate Jillian

The patio outside is Old Florida, but the interior is Old England. Somewhere between the two, does the Chattaway qualify as a diner? Photo by the author.

Frers acquired and gave the restaurant its distinctive style which has been described as "old Florida meets old England."

What that translates to is perhaps the only place in the area where one can sit outside under the Spanish moss enjoying burgers, onion rings, and grilled cheese or enjoy traditional English afternoon tea with crumpets, clotted cream, and preserves inside a dining room that appears to have been transplanted directly from Downing Street.

Jillian and Everett Lund (who passed away in 2002) became the second generation to manage the family business. There have been changes over time, but as of yet those do not include accepting credit cards—to this day the establishment is still cash only.

Angel's Dining Car in Palatka is considered the oldest in Florida, but another worth visiting in the Tampa Bay area is Bob's Train in Sarasota.

1967

Oldest Video Arcade

Treasure Island Fun Center

7770 Seminole Blvd., Seminole, FL 33772

Anyone who has grown up in the Tampa Bay area over the last 50 years has likely had some occasion to visit Treasure Island Fun Center, be it for a family activity, a birthday party, a date night, or simple curiosity about what sort of entertainment fills the 16,000-square-foot space. What visitors discover there is a portal to the not-so-distant past with pool tables, a pizza counter, and an impressive array of arcade games ranging from old-school ticket-generating skee ball machines to pinball, video games, and the latest in virtual reality (VR).

The business is managed today by Clearwater native Jenny Noell. Noell's father, Robert, acquired it in 1998 from Ernestine Tolisano, who co-founded it with her husband. Things have changed a good bit sine the fun center opened, not least of which is that the establishment relocated from Treasure Island to Seminole in January of 2007.

Treasure Island Fun Center is old enough to have experienced the rise, fall, and rebirth of video arcades. The late 1970s into the early 1980s is often considered the Golden Age of coin-operated video games, but with the proliferation of personal computers and home video game consoles, and despite a resurgence during the 1990s, many arcades found that they had become the very thing they offered players—tokens of the past. Treasure Island Fun Center has succeeded where others failed to adapt, which

Treasure Island Fun Center features plenty of old-school classics including skee ball, air hockey, pool tables, and vintage arcade games. Photo by the author.

has meant moving from tokens to debit and credit cards, and reopening after a two-month hiatus during the pandemic.

When asked about the games she enjoys most, Noell says that as a child of the '80s, it's the old classics like Frogger and Spy-Hunter. She was saddened to have to part with their Galaga machine, but is consoled by the fact they still have a working original Ms. Pac-Man. While nostalgia may bring some through the doors, the business itself is looking to the future for ways to keep leveling up its game.

Other popular video game arcades in the area include Lowry Parcade (which also features a craft beer bar) and the Replay Amusement Museum in Tarpon Springs.

1968

Oldest Independent Weekly Newspaper

The *Gabber Newspaper* (formerly the *Gulfport Gabber*)

2908-B, Beach Blvd. S., Gulfport, FL 33707

On October 12, 1910, the City of Gulfport was formed (previously it had been Veteran City, Bonifacio, and Disston City) and almost immediately, the *Tampa Bay Times* made vocal its opposition to the new city's existence in a blistering article. The short-term effect, presumably, was that *Times* subscriptions plummeted among Gulfport residents. Longer-term, the city came to embrace its outsider status as a point of pride. Sometimes though, even outsiders hunger for an advocate and a voice.

When that voice arrived 58 years later, it belonged to George Brann, who used it to lambast Gulfport City Council. Those first weekly editions of his *Gulfport Gabber* had all the production quality of zines printed by college students in the 1980s, but perhaps it was that lack of a polished, professional look that quickly earned it a loyal following. With a readership and a base of advertisers, Brann was able to expand his lone voice into a chorus by adding features, community news, and events.

The *Gabber* passed from Brann to Ted and Elsie Havness in 1980 and then to Ken and Deb Reichart in 1992. The new owners hired a journalist who had just moved to Gulfport and quit a full-time job. Thus Cathy Salustri began a 13-year run as a staff

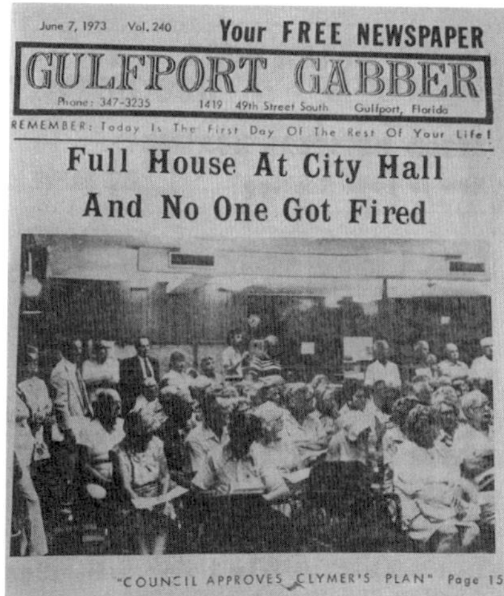

June 7, 1973 Vol. 240 Your FREE NEWSPAPER

GULFPORT GABBER

Phone: 347-3235 1419 49th Street South Gulfport, Florida

REMEMBER: Today Is The First Day Of The Rest Of Your Life!

Full House At City Hall And No One Got Fired

"COUNCIL APPROVES CLYMER'S PLAN" Page 15

The Gabber *Newspaper has come a long way in terms of production quality from early editions like the one shown here. Photo courtesy of Cathy Salustri.*

writer at the *Gabber*. Eventually she returned to freelance work, published a book about Florida backroads travel, and enjoyed a successful writing career. When she learned from her former employer in early 2020 that the *Gabber* was on the verge of closing, Salustri half-jokingly expressed interested in acquiring it. After she and her husband, Barry, reviewed the financials with their accountant, that's exactly what they did.

Their first paper issue appeared in July of 2020 at a time when locals were thankful to have some semblance of normalcy during the pandemic. Since then, the *Gabber* has continued to print, launched digital newsletters, and grown both its staff and readership. Salustri credits the *Gabber*'s hyper-local coverage (the kind now quickly vanishing from larger dailies) for having made it the longest-running independent weekly newspaper in Florida.

Salustri's book Backroads of Paradise *is a great resource for those looking to discover for themselves what people mean when they talk about "Old Florida."*

1977

Oldest Artist Retreat

The Blueberry Patch

4923 20th Ave. S., Gulfport, FL 33707

Amidst constant change, some neighborhoods still manage to cultivate and retain a distinct personality. Gulfport, for example, is decidedly quirky and creative, thanks in large part to one of its most memorable residents, Dallas Laverne Bohrer.

Bohrer, an interior designer by trade, arrived in the area during the mid-1970s to assist his brother in designing a resort. Instead, he turned several acres on 31st Street South in St. Petersburg into an outsider artist haven where likeminded individuals could pursue a life free of conventional constraints. Some came for an afternoon, while others set up camp there for years. Despite occasional friction with the city (which closed down their roadside vegetable stand), the experiment thrived.

Bohrer's passions spanned marijuana and sake consumption as well as recycling and reuse, the latter of which led him to pioneer "palletology"—making furniture from discarded wooden pallets. He coined the term "sharevival" to describe the world he envisioned, and his belief in numerology led him to officially establish "The Blueberry Patch" on the seventh day of the seventh month of 1977 (even today volunteers begin work at exactly 11:11).

The Patch pulled up its roots and moved for a time to Marry Pier in Pass-a-Grille. In 1993, while Bohrer was once again seeking a new permanent home. He discovered a cabin and

Volunteers and board members keep founder Dallas Bohrer's vision alive. Events are held on the first, 7th, 11th and 22nd of each month based on the meaning of those numbers in the I-Ching.

large property in Gulfport next to a storage space where he was temporarily housing the Blueberry Patch. For $45,000 he acquired the property and cabin where he lived for the next decade. In 1993 the Patch sprung up at yet another location on 20th Ave. S., which was once again transformed into the sort of brightly colored visual cacophony that one might imagine from a partnership between Howard Finster and Timothy Leary.

In 2012 Bohrer was recognized with the Spirit of Gulfport award. The following year he moved to a nursing home, where he passed away in 2014. The Blueberry Patch has since become more structured as a 501(c)3 nonprofit organization with a board of directors and bank account. After a two-year hiatus, it reopened in June of 2021 with local performers, vendors, and a new pavilion with functioning restrooms.

Does the Blueberry Patch really qualify as an artist retreat? Maybe a creative space, music venue, and community gathering place would be more accurate. Whatever one calls it, it's something to see.

1996

Oldest Microbrewery

Dunedin Brewery

937 Douglas Ave., Dunedin, FL 34698

The story of brewing in the Tampa Bay area is one of fits, starts, and extended pauses in between, making it a very long road from the "black drink" made by indigenous people (more for ceremonial than recreational purposes) to the area's earliest breweries. These first breweries included Vicente Martinez Ybor's own Florida Brewing Company, which quickly became a leading producer up until Prohibition put an end to its dominance (but not its production, which the Volstead Act could stymie but not halt). In the decades following the repeal of Prohibition, larger breweries (notably Anheuser-Busch and Schlitz) dominated the market and drove out smaller competitors. In the shadow of these bloated beer baronies, however, a local revolution was quietly fermenting.

Enter Michael Norman Bryant, one of several individuals who developed a passion for home-brewing in the 1980s. His interests led him to establish the Dunedin Brewers Guild as a club for other local brewers to collaborate and hone their skills. Out of the froth of this incubator, Bryant and his family officially established Dunedin Brewery. By 2001 it had outgrown its original space and moved to its current location on Douglas Avenue. The same year they moved to their present-day home, Dunedin Brewery joined the victorious legislative battle to overturn Florida's restrictive bottle laws, allowing for the great diversity of microbreweries the sunshine state enjoys today.

Dunedin Brewery earns recognition here for making history, but they also make an impressive assortment of award-winning beers. Photo by the author.

Dunedin Brewery has since added food to its menu and continues to serve as a local lynchpin of the brewing community, fostering frequent collaborations (especially with neighboring 7venth Sun) and spearheading multiple events throughout the year such as Tampa Bay Beer Week. The torch of leadership has been passed to Michael Bryant Senior's son, Michael Lyn Bryant. He today employs nearly 50 individuals and continues the family tradition of innovation with side projects like the much-loved—if short-lived—quirky, small-batch Antibrewery (which closed in 2020 due to COVID-19).

Coming up on its 26th year in business, Dunedin Brewery holds the dual title of oldest microbrewery in the Tampa Bay area and oldest in the state of Florida.

To learn more about Dunedin's history, from its Scottish heritage to its once booming citrus industry, visitors should stop by the Dunedin History Museum.

1997

Oldest Paranormal Investigators

SPIRITS of St. Petersburg

10 5th St. N., St. Petersburg, FL 33701

In the 1970s and '80s, ghost hunting and paranormal investigations were fringe activities, just beginning to filter into the general culture through films like *Poltergeist* and *Ghostbusters*. In the '90s paranormal investigation received a boost from the success of the TV show *The X-Files*. By the mid-2000s there was an overwhelming interest in and acceptance of professional paranormal investigation, driven largely by *Ghost Hunters* and dozens of similar shows, which brought the concept fully into the American mainstream.

Of the early paranormal investigative groups, clubs, and businesses, the vast majority have passed on. Of the dozens that operate currently within the greater Tampa Bay area, the oldest continually active team is SPIRITS of St. Petersburg, led by Brandy Stark, PhD.

As a child, Stark was equally fascinated and frightened by ghosts. Her college studies led to a deeper exploration of cultural, religious, and historical perspectives on death and the afterlife. She began working at the University of South Florida St. Petersburg campus library,

Shown here is an image from an investigation of Haslam's Books. (Opposite page) Brandy Stark, PhD, founder of SPIRITS of St. Petersburg. Photos courtesy of Brandy Stark, PhD.

where she was able to read more about local ghost stories and conduct her first investigations at the Nelson Poynter Library (now Davis Hall) and the Williams House. She also began connecting online with more experienced investigators who helped guide and mentor her.

She officially launched SPIRITS in 1997 and published her first article on the paranormal in the *Crow's Nest* in 1999. During a talk on the paranormal in 2000, she met others interested in the field and the team was born, officially incorporating in 2004. Since then she has conducted as many as 400 investigations with a team that has expanded and contracted over two decades. From her office at ArtLofts (which is itself allegedly haunted), she offers investigative services as well as local ghost tours. Some of the more memorable locations she's explored include the Tampa Bay Theater, Haslam's Bookstore, and Rose Cemetery.

To what does Stark owe the longevity of SPIRITS? Selectivity in the cases she signs on for, consistency in the tools and methodologies she uses, and above all, being ethical and honest in presenting her findings.

Stark has captured some of the area's tales from beyond the grave in her book, Supernatural St. Petersburg & Paranormal Pinellas.

2015

Oldest Escape Room

Tampa Bay Escape Room

625 Cleveland St., Clearwater, FL 33755

For being a comparatively recent phenomenon, escape rooms have spread throughout Florida and the Tampa Bay area with a speed that would impress any invasive species. The idea actually goes back to the text-based computer games of the 1980s like John Wilson's *Behind Closed Doors*. As graphics evolved, so did these often themed "escape the room" games, through which players progressed by finding clues and solving riddles or puzzles. In 2004 Toshimitsu Takagi released the massively popular *Crimson Room*, and three years later Takao Kato is credited with having created the first real life version, birthing a new industry. One could argue that Disney's Haunted Mansion also deserves some credit for having planted the idea in the heads of its guests, who are encouraged by the narrator upon entering to consider how they will leave a room with no windows or doors.

Various themed rooms challenge teams to find clues, solve puzzles, and beat the clock. Photo courtesy of Tampa Bay Escape Room.

Escape rooms were a hit and started showing up in strip malls and store fronts everywhere. The first of these in the Tampa Bay area opened in 2015 and was an immediate success. Even seasoned players like Gil Bakshi and his wife were impressed with the attention to detail and immersive storytelling they experienced there in 2019. They had started their own escape room the year before, but when they learned from the owner that she was planning to sell the business, they jumped at the opportunity.

The business changed hands in early 2019, just as COVID-19 swept through the country. After the first few months of quarantine, no doubt many Americans began to feel like their own homes had become escape rooms. Understandably, some of these businesses have opted not to reopen, but Tampa Bay Escape Room has resumed its regular schedule, open weekday nights and weekends. Players can test their wits in Wizard's Keep, which challenges apprentices to free their master from an interdimensional prison; Kidnapped, which gives players one hour to escape before their captors return; or Cabin in the Woods, in which groups discover that the cabin they have taken shelter in is more dangerous than the storm raging outside.

According to industry reports, as of February 2021 there were 2,080 escape rooms in the United States, which is down from 2,250 in August of 2020.

MANATEE AND SARASOTA COUNTIES

1845

Oldest Preserved Plantation House

Gamble Mansion

3708 Northeast, Patten Ave., Ellenton, FL 34222

Following his service in the Second Seminole War, Major Robert Gamble Jr. arrived in Manatee County in 1843 to make use of the Armed Occupation Act, enacted that year, giving 160 acres of land and one year's rations to anyone willing to clear and cultivate the land for five years.

Gamble began work on his plantation and house in 1845, adding 3,300 acres of land in 1847. By 1850 the two-story, red brick, Greek Revival style building was complete and still stands today as the oldest building in Manatee County and the only remaining antebellum plantation house in the southern half of Florida.

Like most plantation owners, Gamble relied heavily on slave labor, from draining and developing the land to operating his sugar mills, which, despite production in the order of tens of thousands of pounds, could not offset the losses incurred from hurricanes, poor market conditions, and crushing debt. He sold the plantation in 1859 to John Cofield and Robert Davis for $190,000.

According to the 1869 census, Cofield owned 190 slaves ranging in age from two months to 105 years old occupying 57 slave houses (none of which remain). At the start of the Civil

The antebellum Gamble Mansion plantation house as it looked in this 1936 Burgert Brothers photo, courtesy of the Tampa-Hillsborough County Public Library System.

War, Cofield and Davis ceased making mortgage payments and the plantation became a confederate depot. Blockade runner Captain Archibald McNeill and his family took up residence there in 1862 and two years later a Union raiding party destroyed the grist mill, ending production at the plantation.

Gamble Mansion had one more unique role to play in the Civil War. Following the capture of Jefferson Davis, Confederate Secretary of State Judah P. Benjamin made his way to Florida and hid at Gamble Mansion while he arranged passage to England via Nassau and Havana.

After the war, the mansion fell into a state of decay for decades. In 1925 the Daughters of the Confederacy purchased the mansion, but turned it over to the State of Florida, which has restored and preserved it ever since.

Visitors should be aware that while the site is managed by the Florida State Park system, it is also home to the Judah P. Benjamin Confederate Memorial.

1860

Oldest Preserved County Courthouse

Manatee County Courthouse

1404 Manatee Ave. E., Bradenton, FL 34208

The Armed Occupation Act of 1842 offered cheap land to those with an adventurous spirit (and a loaded gun), as a means of taming the Florida frontier. It enticed some, such as the Braden brothers (for whom Bradenton is named) and the Gates Family. Others followed suit and in 1855, Manatee County separated from Hillsborough, with an area spanning 5,000 square miles (south to Charlotte Harbor and east to Lake Okeechobee). As a new county, one of Manatee's first orders of business was establishing a place to conduct Manatee County's business, which is to say, a courthouse.

Josiah and Mary Gates, the first permanent white settlers in the Village of Manatee, offered some of their land for the purpose of constructing a courthouse and jail. In 1858, a committee elected

Within Manatee Village, the courthouse has been restored to its original appearance and layout. Photos by the author.

to pay Ezekiel Glazier $5 to produce plans and $700 to build both buildings. Over objections about the fact that Glazier was himself part of the selection committee, the courthouse was completed in 1860 (without the jail).

Although the courthouse only served its intended purpose for six years, they were consequential ones during which the country's official definition of "property" ceased to include other human beings. In 1866, the county seat moved to a more central location and the original courthouse became a church, then a parsonage, a social hall, and finally a private home.

By 1975 the Manatee United Methodist Church planned to demolish the old courthouse, but a group of citizens formed the Heritage of Manatee's Environment (HOME) Committee (subsequently re-formed as the Manatee County Historical Commission) to rescue and relocate the structure. The church agreed to donate the building, which became the first of now 14 points of interest within Manatee Village Historical Park.

Removing the flooring and siding revealed the original wood and allowed the jury room and judge's chambers to be reconstructed as they were originally. It was reopened to the public in 1976 and includes a desk handmade by Josiah Gates, old maps, and other historical artifacts.

Today the building is considered the oldest wooden structure originally designed as a courthouse in Florida.

The remains of "Braden Castle" can also be found a mile and a half from Manatee Village, fenced off in the center of a mobile home community.

1902

Oldest Commercial Ice House

Metro/Manatee Ice Co.

808 8th Ave. Dr. W., Bradenton, FL 34205

Few who've spent a sweltering summer in the Tampa Bay area can fail to appreciate the modern marvels of air conditioning and refrigeration, which trace back to Dr. John Gorrie. While seeking a means of reducing the fevers of malaria patients in Apalachicola, he invented an "ice machine" which earned the first US patent for mechanical refrigeration in 1851. In 1902 Willis Carrier developed the first modern electrical air conditioning unit.

Prior to the widespread adoption of these cooling technologies, Floridians relied on ice houses to keep perishable foods fresh for storage and transportation. This was especially important for farming and fishing communities like Bradenton.

Little is known by the current owners about the origin of their ice house, save that it has been in operation since at least 1902—possibly earlier—and it is rumored to have been owned by one of Bradenton's early mayors. In the 1970s it was acquired from a Sarasota farm by Wayne Morgan, who operated the business until he retired in the late 1980s. Doug, one of his three sons, continues to own and manage it today.

In some ways the business has remained unchanged—they supply fishing and shrimping boats (including Red Lobster's local fleet) with ice from time to time. They are also one of the very

The brick exterior of the Manatee/Metro Ice Co. in 2022 looks much the same way it has for over a century. Photo by the author.

few that still produces ice in 300-pound blocks. Those blocks find a variety of uses including ice sculptures (Doug personally carves the sculptures for the annual Vince Lombardi Award Ceremony).

In other ways, the business has adapted to the times—gone is the train which used run past the ice house where it would fill up with ice to keep produce cool. Today they produce wholesale crushed and cubed ice, which ends up in the freezers of convenience stores like Racetrack, 7-Eleven, and Wawa. They also provide ice from the dock to local food trucks, and they have a machine which makes snow for a variety of parties and winter events. Deemed an "essential business," they have kept their doors open and local ice boxes full throughout the COVID-19 pandemic.

Among those ice houses that have been repurposed is the one built in 1920 in Anna Maria Island, which is now home to the Anna Maria Island Historical Society Museum.

1910

Oldest Sarasota Celebrity Estate

Historic Spanish Point

337 N. Tamiami Trl., Osprey, FL 34229

Fame is an ever-evolving concept. It clearly includes famous authors like Stephen King and Tim Dorsey, athletes (Babe Zaharias, Derek Jeeter, and Tom Brady for instance), wrestling stars-turned actors (Hulk Hogan and Dave Bautista), sports announcers like Dick Vitale, the circus performing Wallendas, and those like Carole Baskin, who find themselves in the spotlight of a Netflix series. To this group, all of whom have called the Tampa Bay area home, today one could add anyone with a sufficiently large social media following.

And then there is royalty—if not literally, then in the American sense, meaning business moguls, socialites, heirs and heiresses, and the like. It is to this category that Sarasota's first famous

(Left) View of the Sunken Garden and Pergola. (Right) A statue of Bertha Potter Palmer along one of the paths. Photos by the author.

resident, Bertha Palmer, belongs, and 17 years before the Ringlings and their accompanying circus arrived, she was already transforming the mosquito-infested marshland into the cultured city it has since become.

Word of her arrival on February 24, 1910, was reported in the *Sarasota Times*, which described the Chicago hotel heiress and philanthropist as "one of the widest known American women." If she was bothered by the attention, it didn't prevent her from purchasing 140,000 acres there, where she proceeded to build her winter home and gardens at Historic Spanish Point in Osprey. From here, she helped apply the latest in agricultural science such as canal systems for drainage at Bee Ridge along with research and practices that revolutionized the area's ranching, which was still being conducted much like the Spanish centuries earlier.

Her stamp was not the first on the winter estate she created at Spanish Point—it had shell middens and burial mounds possibly as old as 3,000 B.C.E., as well as some of the structures built by John and Eliza Webb, who moved there from New York in 1867, claiming 145 acres under the Federal Homestead Act.

Although the mansion that Palmer built nearby has since been demolished, and much of the land she once owned has been developed, the multiple gardens she cultivated there remain open to the public today as part of Selby Gardens.

Another of Bertha Palmer's innovations: the brownie, which originated in the kitchen of the Palmer House hotel in Chicago and was served at the Columbian Exposition World's Fair in 1893.

1915

Oldest Family-Owned Department Store Chain

Beall's

700 13th Ave. E., Bradenton, FL 34208

The story of the Tampa Bay area over time is also a story of changing consumer trends and the rise of department stores. Maas Brothers opened in 1886 and expanded to 39 locations before being swallowed in 1991 by the Burdines chain. Then there was the massive Webb's City in St. Petersburg, the self-proclaimed "World's Most Unusual Drug Store," credited with introducing the express checkout lane concept. Of these early retail pioneers, however, the prize for longevity goes to Bradenton-based Bealls.

The story begins in 1915, when the 22-year-old Robert M. Beall opened a dry goods store along the Manatee River, which he named the Dollar Limit, as nothing in the store cost more than one dollar (until after World War I, when the pricing and store name changed to the V Dollar Limit). In 1924 he built a second store and though the bank took ownership of his business during the Great Depression, he was able to repurchase it in 1944.

Robert's son E. R. joined the business in 1940 and six years later they changed the business name to Beall's Department Store, which Robert continued to run until shortly before his death. In the 1950s E. R. glimpsed the future in the shopping centers that spang up to serve middle- and fixed-income customers.

Egbert Beall with RM and Robert Beall in 1970. Photo courtesy of the Manatee County Public Library System.

He expanded Beall's first within Bradenton and then in Venice. In 1962, the company generated over a million dollars in sales.

Bob Beall, E. R.'s son, became the third generation to join the business in 1970. When Bob became president of the company 10 years later, it had become a true chain, producing $38 million in annual sales. Bob was joined by his son Matt in 2004. In 2015 the company's centennial was celebrated with a documentary, a mural and historical marker at the site of the first store, and other such activities.

Today, the company has thousands of employees at over 500 stores, generating over a billion dollars annually. Despite temporary closures for COVID-19, it appears that the sky rather than the dollar is the true limit to the chain's continued success.

There is another unrelated chain named Beall's (3 Bealls Holding Corp.) in Texas. When its parent company filed for bankruptcy in 2020, Florida's Beall's purchased the right to use their name.

1923

OLDEST MINOR LEAGUE BASEBALL STADIUM

LECOM PARK (FORMERLY MCKECHNIE FIELD, BRAVES FIELD, NINTH STREET PARK, AND CITY PARK)

1611 9th Street West, Bradenton, FL

So symbiotic is the relationship between baseball spring training and the Tampa Bay area that it's difficult to imagine one without the other. How strong is that connection? A list of the area's spring training teams includes the New York Yankees, the Philadelphia Phillies, the Toronto Blue Jays, and the Baltimore Orioles. Al Lang Stadium, named for a former St. Petersburg Mayor who was instrumental in bringing the boys of summer to town, lives on as a MLB stadium for the Rowdies. More recently, the Tampa Baseball Museum has opened in the former Ybor City home of Al Lopez.

It is the Pittsburg Pirates, however, who have their Spring season in the area's oldest minor league/spring training stadium (and second oldest in the country), LECOM Park in Bradenton. The distinctly Florida Spanish Mission style architecture of the park, which features white stucco on the main grandstand, does not diminish its nostalgic appeal for baseball park enthusiasts, some of whom consider it Florida's own Fenway Park.

Before the stadium was erected, it was the site of Ninth Street Park (where the Bradenton Growers played). On December 9, 2019 Manatee County voted to bring major baseball south of

A 1977 aerial view of McKechnie Field on 9th Street West in Bradenton. Photo courtesy of the Manatee County Public Library System.

St. Petersburg for the first time. Business owner Robert M. Beall Sr. played a part in coaxing the St. Louis Cardinals from their spring training site in Orange Texas. The Cardinals played there just one year before the Philadelphia Phillies took their place until 1928, when they were followed by the Boston Red Sox. The Cardinals returned to the stadium in the 1930s and the Boston Bees (Atlanta Braves) played there up until the field was used as a military training base during World War II.

When baseball resumed, the Boston Braves made their spring home there until 1963, during which time the field was renamed for Baseball Hall of Fame manager and Bradenton-native Bill McKechnie. In 1968, the Pirates agreed to a 40-year lease. Major renovations in the 1990s helped extend the relationship with the Pirates until at least 2037.

In 2010 minor league baseball returned to the stadium for the first time since 1926 in the form of Pirates affiliate, the Bradenton Marauders.

1949

Oldest Youth Circus

The Sailor Circus

2075 Bahia Vista St., Sarasota, FL 34239

When John and Mable Ringling bought their winter home in Sarasota in 1912, the population was somewhere just north of 840 residents. In 1927, a year after John's brother Charles died, the Ringling Circus officially relocated to Sarasota, forever altering the city's trajectory. Although John Ringling's later years were marked by grief over the loss of his wife, a brief and failed second marriage, and a series of business blunders that left him all but penniless, perhaps the truest measure of his wealth is in the creative legacy that has continued to shape "Circus City."

The Sailor Circus is a prime example of that ongoing impact. In 1949, 13 years after John Ringling died of pneumonia, Sarasota High School established a small gym class focused on the circus arts. The following year the class relocated to the football field to accommodate demand and by 1952, the program's scope had expanded to include more complex open-air aerial acts. That same year it was featured in a 30-minute Warner Bros. picture short, which brought the fledgling Sailor Circus national and international recognition. With the help of James A. Haley, it secured for itself a variation of Ringling Brothers Barnum & Bailey's tag line as "The Greatest Little Show on Earth."

Television appearances and traveling performances ensued. By 1967 the Sailor Circus had outgrown the school that birthed

Children try tightrope walking at the Sarasota High School Sailor Circus. Department of Commerce photograph from 1952. Image number C016209. Photo courtesy of the State Archives of Florida, Florida Memory.

it and graduated to its own permanent location on Bahia Vista Street. Here it was adopted by Circus Sarasota and is now part of the Circus Arts Conservatory (CAC).

In 2019 the CAC unveiled its $4.5 million renovation of the Sailor Circus Arena, which coincided with the 70th anniversary of the Sailor Circus. With roughly 3,000 seats and over 28,000 square feet of indoor space, the program is poised to continue engaging fourth through twelfth grade student performers and their fans. Even as one by one, the old, big-name, big-top shows pack up and vanish into the vintage Americana sunset, the Sailor Circus is still going strong.

For more on circus history visitors can check out the Ringling Circus Museum as well as the International Independent Showman's Museum in Riverview.

1953

Oldest Antique Car Museum

Sarasota Classic Car Museum

5500 N. Tamiami Trl., Sarasota, FL 34243

The story of the Tampa Bay area can read as a modern romance . . . of that enduringly and quintessentially American love affair between Americans and their automobiles. In 1914 Henry Ford himself, after a visit to the winter estate of fellow inventor Thomas Edison in Fort Myers, bought the home next door. Around that same time the "tin-can tourists" were paving the way to transforming the Florida Landscape. In the 1920s and '30s Florida's Daytona Beach became the center of the racing world (today NASCAR season typically opens with the Firestone Grand Prix in St. Petersburg). In 1954 drag racing pioneer "Big Daddy" Don Garlits built his first car in North Tampa.

Of the many automobile museums throughout the area, Sarasota Classic Car Museum is not only the oldest in the state but also the second-oldest continually operating in the country.

After a trip to the area in the early 1950s, brothers Herbert and Bob Horn decided that Sarasota was the ideal spot to relocate their car collection from Fort Dodge, Iowa. In March of 1953 they opened "Horn's Cars of Yesterday" with over 70 vehicles on display, including an 1897 Duryea Buggyaut, John Ringling's own 1914 Rolls Royce Town Car, and Mable Ringling's Pierce Arrow.

John Ringling's Rolls Royce Silver Ghost is just one of the many rare vehicles on display at the Sarasota Classic Car Museum. Photos by the author.

The museum was a success out of the starting block with an 87 percent increase in visitor traffic from 1954 to 1955. The brothers added a Nickelodeon Room, a Music Box Arcade, a cycle collection, a blacksmith shop, and other features.

In 1967 Walter Bellm bought and expanded the museum to include his own collection of over 20 antique cars. Bellm in turn sold the museum to Martin Godbey in 1997. Once Godbey was in the driver's seat, he again renovated the building (which is over 50,000 square feet) and added yet more exotic cars to the collection, including a Don Garlits dragster. Like most businesses, the museum had to shift gears during the COVID-19 pandemic, but it has since resumed its regular hours and has no intention of putting the brakes on its operation anytime soon.

Anyone driven to spend a day among vintage vehicles should also visit both the Tampa Bay Automobile Museum and the Don Garlits Museum of Drag Racing.

1954

Oldest Tiki Bar

Bahi Hut

4675 N. Tamiami Trl., Sarasota, FL 34234

Thatched huts, ukulele music, leis, surfboards, and of course potent tropical beverages often elaborately garnished—these are some of the quintessential hallmarks of tiki bars and their loyal subculture. The first of these was created in California in 1933 by Ernest Raymond Beaumont Gantt (better know as Donn Beach or Don the Beachcomber). His unique take on South Pacific and Polynesian culture, food, and drink (which included his invention, the Zombie) made his bar a hit. This spawned an industry and competitors such as Vic Bergeron Trader Vic's, which claims credit for inventing the Mai Tai. But the real heyday for Tiki bars came when GIs returned home from the Pacific following World War II, sometimes clad in the aloha shirts they had picked up in Hawaii.

In Florida, perhaps the best known of these bars is Mai-Kai in Fort Lauderdale which featured Polynesian dinner shows (it closed during the COVID-19 pandemic but plans to reopen under new ownership). Mai-Kai, established in 1956, is not the state's oldest tiki bar though. That honor goes to the Bahi Hut in Sarasota, which has been a local fixture connected to the Golden Host Resort since 1954 and puts it among the oldest operating tiki bars in the country.

The exterior of the Bahi Hut and some of the Tiki-style décor inside. Photos by the author.

In true tiki tradition, it has invented its own drink called the Bahi Aloha, which the bar owner describes as a well-concocted drink full of rum and coconut. While they may not have invented the Mai Tai, some say that they've perfected it—their version is so strong that patrons are limited to just two of them.

In 2019 the restaurant went smoke free and in 2021 the hotel remodel was finished, restoring the rooms to their original, mid-century modern feel, down to the bubble microwaves, lounge chairs, and décor. The remodel comes at a good time—as the pandemic winds down, the Bahi Hut has never been busier. Even if it takes a little longer to order a drink, it is worth experiencing a piece of Americana that few bars can hold a candle (or tiki torch) to.

From 1964 until 1980 Indian Shores was home to the South Seas Polynesian theme park, Tiki Gardens, remnants of which are on display at the Indian Rocks Historical Museum.

1960

Oldest Opera Company

Sarasota Opera (Formerly the Asolo Opera Guild)

61 N. Pineapple Ave., Sarasota, FL 34236

From the time he moved to Sarasota until long after his death in 1936, John Ringling's meteoric impact has shaped the area. But that legacy was far from secure at the time of his passing. His finances were a disaster that took a decade for his creditors and family members to sort out. By that time, the state had taken control of his estate and in 1948 appointed Everett 'Chick' Austin Jr. to serve as the Ringling Museum of Art's first director. Under Austin's guidance, Ringling's legacy would continue to flourish, first with the opening of Circus Museum and the acquisition of the Asolo Theatre.

The theater was originally constructed by architect Antonio Locatelli in Asolo, Italy, within the great hall of Caterina Cornaro, Queen of Cyprus. In 1931 it was dismantled and stored in Venice throughout World War II. In 1950 it was acquired by the Ringling Museum for all of $8,000 and shipped to Sarasota, where it was rebuilt and reopened in 1958. But having such a magnificent venue begs the question: Who will perform there?

A partial solution arrived in 1960 when the Turnau Opera Players presented their first season there. A year later the Asolo Opera Guild was established to bring the company back annually and in 1974 the guild began presenting their own productions as the Asolo Opera Company. By 1979 the company was ready

Sarasota Opera House, late March 2008, after complete interior and exterior renovation. Public domain.

for a space all its own. They acquired, renovated, and reopened the historic A. B. Edwards Theater in 1984 as the Sarasota Opera House. Its more recent $20 million historic renovation has led Music America to label it one of the country's best venues for opera.

In 1983 the company brought on Victor DeRenzi, now in his 40th season as artistic director and principal conductor. His focus has extended to training via the Apprentice Artist and Studio Artist programs he founded. Similarly, under his leadership the Sarasota Youth Opera has become one of the most comprehensive in the nation, ensuring that both the Sarasota Opera and, by extension, the gift of John Ringling, will continue for generations to come.

The Historic Asolo Theater and the Sarasota Opera House are just two of the area's many venues. The Van Wezel Performing Arts Hall is another worth visiting.

1964

Oldest Surf Shop

West Coast Surf Shop

3902 Gulf Dr., Holmes Beach, FL 34217

Ron Jon might be the first name most people associate with Florida surf shops. Their 52,000 square foot store in Cocoa Beach claims to be the largest on earth, but they are neither the first nor the oldest to operate in the Sunshine State. That honor belongs to West Coast Surf Shop located in Holmes Beach on Anna Maria Island, where owner Jim Brady has been operating for nearly 60 years.

Brady already had a passion for surfing when his father, a missile-man, moved the family from Texas to Manatee County in 1963. The following year a 16-year-old Brady matriculated at Manatee High School and launched his surf shop with partner Jim Duraddi, who was slightly older. The two caught the wave at the right time and place it seemed; they had steady demand from

Drawing of the original surf shop and photo of the owners in front of their store, courtesy of the Brady family.

the outset and within eight months of opening, Brady bought out his partner.

In the early days the shop's inventory was composed of just boards and wax. That's changed significantly over the years to include men's, women's, and children's sportswear, hats, and other gear. Brady has had other stores in Florida and Puerto Rico, but his first has always been his top performer. In 1969 Brady's wife joined him and continues to manage the store today. More recently the couple has been joined by their daughter, who handles marketing and social media.

Just as the business and the surfing industry have changed, so too has Anna Maria Island. Brady can recall a time when over the course of a day he could count the number of vehicles that drove past his shop on one hand. Now that number might be in the thousands or even tens of thousands during the island's peak season.

The tight-knit local business and surfing circles have kept the business afloat through tough times including the recession in 2008 and an electrical fire in 2018. The shop was able to keep its doors open throughout the pandemic and as of this writing, West Coast Surf Shop's business is cresting at an all-time high.

While not exactly commonplace, Florida's west coast has produced some surfing champions like Logan Hofstetter, who remarked, "if you can surf here, you can surf anywhere."

1978

Oldest Tennis Academy

IMG Academy
(Formerly Nick Bollettieri Tennis Academy)

5650 Bollettieri Blvd., Bradenton, FL 34210

Aspiring tennis players learn early on that the road to Wimbledon is punishingly arduous, prohibitively expensive, and very often runs through the Sunshine State. Some will play at the Tampa Tennis Academy founded by Harry Hopman; others will follow in the footsteps of Andy Roddick, Jennifer Capriati, Maria Sharapova, and both Serena and Venus Williams in Delray Beach through Rick Macci's program; still others attend the Tampa Bay area's oldest academy founded by Nick Bollettieri, whose students have included Mary Pierce, Anna Kournikova, and Andre Agassi among others.

Originally from Pelham, New York, Bollettieri graduated with a philosophy degree from Spring Hill College, rose to the rank of First Lieutenant in the US Army, and studied at University of Miami Law School before finding his calling as a trainer.

In 1977 he moved to Longboat Key and instructed tennis at the Colony Beach and Tennis Resort for a year before opening his own Nick Bollettieri Tennis Academy (BTA) on 40 acres of land near Bradenton in Manatee County. To the area's long list of pioneers one more name can be added, for it was here that Bollettieri is credited with having established the first major tennis boarding school, forever altering the manner in which elite junior players are trained.

(Left) Areal view of the Bollettieri Sports Academy from 1998. (right) Nick Bollettieri with students at the Bollettieri Sports Academy Open House in 1998. Photos courtesy of the Manatee County Public Library System.

In 1987 International Management Group (IMG) purchased the academy, to which it added the David Leadbetter Golf Academy in 1993, soccer and baseball programs in 1994, hockey and basketball by 2001, and the John Madden Football Academy in 2010. In thc fall of 2020, IMG Academy broke ground on a new tennis complex featuring clay and hard stadium courts, four outdoor red clay courts, five indoor courts, meeting rooms, office space, and its own hall of fame.

Visitors might even catch nonagenarian Bollettieri himself there from time to time, as he is still actively involved in training. Of course, he also has books and DVDs, and has netted some impressive recognitions. These include induction into the International Tennis Hall of Fame in 2014 and the being first white man inducted into the Black Tennis Hall of Fame in 2015.

The documentary Love Means Zero *gives a deeper look at Bollettieri, including his relationship with Andre Agassi, which remains a sore subject for both men.*

1981

Oldest Bird Sanctuary and Wildlife Rehab Facility

Save Our Seabirds (Formerly the Pelican Man's Bird Sanctuary)

1708 Ken Thompson Pkwy., Sarasota, FL 34236

Today there are dozens of wildlife sanctuaries throughout the area, but in 1981 that was far from the case. Dale Shields, who sold cars for 25 years in Flint, Michigan, before retiring to Sarasota's Golden Gate neighborhood, discovered this firsthand when he found an injured pelican on the shore. He brought the bird home and searched for rehabilitation resources at the local, state, and federal level—all to no avail. So he took matters into his own hands and, with the help of a veterinarian friend, nursed the bird back to health. Thus was born the "Pelican Man" and his bird sanctuary.

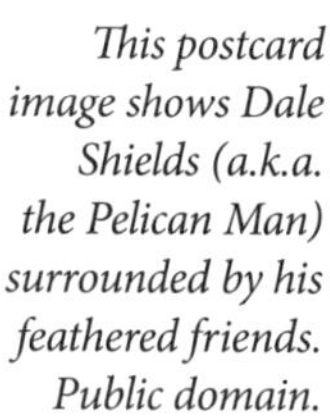

This postcard image shows Dale Shields (a.k.a. the Pelican Man) surrounded by his feathered friends. Public domain.

Over the next several years Dale rescued more birds as well as possums, racoons, turtles, squirrels, and essentially any animal that he could, until two things happened. The first was that he simply ran out of room in his garage, and the second was that he was well on his way to burning through his retirement savings.

He negotiated with the City of Sarasota to lease three acres at the sanctuary's current location for $1 per year. Following an article in *Parade Magazine*, donations began to flow in, enabling him to build permanent enclosures and expand his staff. In 1990 he was recognized as one of President George Bush's "1,000 Points of Light." But the Pelican Man's health declined, and he passed away in 2003. Three years later the facility shut down for lack of funding.

Enter Lee Fox, who was seeking a new location for her "Save Our Seabirds" organization when she came across the Pelican Man's bird sanctuary. With financial support from a benefactor, she was able to pay the $30,000 the city required and reopen the facility under its new name. Since then, the organization has grown to 14 staff members and over 60 volunteers who care for 130 non-releasable birds and respond to roughly 5,000 animal emergencies each year. The facility was closed for 16 months due to COVID-19, but since reopening in July of 2021, an average of 2,200 visitors flock to the sanctuary each week.

Today there are many places where injured birds can get help. A short list includes Tampa Bay Raptor Rescue, Seaside Seabird Sanctuary, and Birds of Paradise Sanctuary & Rescue.

SOURCES

Oldest Map of the Tampa Bay Area
Leto, Manny. "Earliest Known Map of Florida Goes on Display at Tampa Bay History Center." Tampa Bay History Center, *83 Degrees*, September 10, 2020. https://www.83degreesmedia.com/inthenews/earliest-map-of-Florida-debuts-at-Tampa-Bay-History-Center-091020.aspx; Wikipedia contributors. "1757 Tampa expedition." *Wikipedia, The Free Encyclopedia*. https://en.wikipedia.org/w/index.php?title=1757_Tampa_expedition&oldid=1093192239 (accessed June 30, 2022); "1757 Tampa Expedition Explained." *Everything Explained: Today*, 2022. https://everything.explained.today/1757_Tampa_expedition/

Oldest Single-Story Family Home
"This Old House." Tampa Pix website. http://www.tampapix.com/oldesthouse.htm; Guzzo, Paul. "The Oldest House in Tampa Area Has Moved." *Tampa Bay Times*, February 15, 2018.; Guzzo, Paul. "Want to Own History? The Oldest House in Tampa Is for Sale." *Tampa Bay Times*, July 29, 2021.

Oldest Shipyard
Jean Street Shipyard website, http://jeanstreetshipyard.net; Wikipedia contributors. "Jean Street Shipyard." *Wikipedia, The Free Encyclopedia*. https://en.wikipedia.org/w/index.php?title=Jean_Street_Shipyard&oldid=986503877 (accessed June 30, 2022).

Oldest Lighthouse
"Egmont Key Lighthouse." LighthouseFriends.com. https://www.lighthousefriends.com/light.asp?ID=370

Oldest Public Cemetery
"Oaklawn Cemetery," The Historical Marker Database. https://www.hmdb.org/m.asp?m=135974; Wikipedia contributors. "Oaklawn Cemetery." *Wikipedia, The Free Encyclopedia*. https://en.wikipedia.org/w/index.php?title=Oaklawn_Cemetery&oldid=1052242410 (accessed June 30, 2022).; Roberson, Bender Shelby Jean, and Elizabeth Laramie Dunham. *Tampa's Historic Cemeteries*. Charleston, SC: Arcadia Publishing, 2013.

Oldest Masonic Lodge
"Hillsborough Lodge History," Hillsborough Lodge No.25, https://www.hillsborough25.org/lodge_history.html; Rajtar, Steve. *A Guide to Historic Tampa Florida*. Charleston, SC: The History Press, 2007.

Oldest African American Baptist Congregation
"A History of BBIC & Significant Events." https://www.bbictampa.com/history; Castor, Kathy, U.S. Representative, Speeches and Floor Statements. "Beulah Baptist Institutional Church." Washington D. C., August 20, 2015. https://castor.house.gov/news/documentsingle.aspx?DocumentID=398106

Oldest Public High School
Wikipedia contributors. "Hillsborough High School (Tampa, Florida)." *Wikipedia, The Free Encyclopedia*. https://en.wikipedia.org/w/index.php?title=Hillsborough_High_School_(Tampa,_Florida)&oldid=1087803258 (accessed July 1, 2022).; "The Eight Homes of Hillsborough High School." Tampa Pix. https://tampapix.com/HHS.htm

Oldest Law Firm
"Our History." Macfarlane, Ferguson & McMullen website. https://www.mfmlegal.com/our-history/; Pinder, Ashley. "Chester H. Ferguson." UF Law website, June 27,, 2014. https://www.law.ufl.edu/alumni/chester-h-ferguson

Oldest Elementary School
"The History of John Gorrie Elementary School." Gorrie Elementary School website. https://www.hillsboroughschools.org/domain/2826#:~:text=John%20Gorrie%20Elementary%20School%2C%20the,3%20stood%20in%20later%20years; Rajtar, Steve. *A Guide to Historic Tampa Florida*. Charleston, SC: The History Press, 2007.

Oldest Phosphate Mining Operation
"The Peace River: The discovery of phosphate." Southwest Florida Water Management District website. https://www4.swfwmd.state.fl.us/peaceriver/phosphate.php#:~:text=Francis%20LeBaron%20of%20the%20U.S.,company%20and%20commenced%20mining%20operations; Wikipedia contributors. "Bone Valley." *Wikipedia, The Free Encyclopedia*. https://en.wikipedia.org/w/index.php?title=Bone_Valley&oldid=1093192236 (accessed July 1, 2022).

Oldest Elevator
Floridian Elevators Youtube Video. "OLDEST LIFT IN FLORIDA: MANUALLY CONTROLLED 1891 Otis Elevator at Henry B. Plant Hall, Tampa, FL." December 25, 2018. https://www.youtube.com/watch?v=pgWUroZqGDE

Oldest Public Botanical Garden
"Henry B. Plant Park." Henry B. Plant Museum website. https://www.plantmuseum.com/about/plant-park; Gottlieb, Sarah. "Plant Park's rich history brought to life with audio tour." *Tampa Bay Times*, April 3, 2013.; Kelley, McKenna. "Four Quintessential Pieces of Tampa Public Art." *Tampa Magazine*. May 19, 2020. https://tampamagazines.com/4-quintessential-pieces-of-tampa-public-art

Oldest Jewish Congregation
Heimovics, Rachel B., and Zerivitz, Marchia. "Florida Jewish Heritage Trail." A Florida Heritage Publication, Florida Department of State, Division of Historical Resources, 2020.; Lesser, Stephanie. "Tampa's Oldest Conservative Jewish Congregation Marked by Plaque." *Patch*, Tampa, FL, July 26, 2011.; "Our History." Congregation Schaarai Zedek website. https://www.zedek.org/who-we-are/our-history/; Weiss, Kevin. "Exploring Tampa's Jewish history." *The Laker* / Lutz News, November 1, 2017.

Oldest Italian Market
Pizzo, Tony. "The Italian Heritage in Tampa." Scholar Commons, University of South Florida, *Sunland Tribune*, Volume 3, Article 6, 1977. https://digitalcommons.usf.edu/cgi/viewcontent.cgi?article=1022&context=sunlandtribune; Wood, Sara (Interviewer), Mitchum, Deborah (Transcription). "Transcript of interview with Mark Cacciatore, Cacciatore and Sons Italian Meat Market & Deli, February 11, 2015. https://qy9t02v0kj93v7vro1461moj-wpengine.netdna-ssl.com/wp-content/uploads/cacciatore-mark_sfa-wood_11feb2015.pdf; Daly, Sean. "Historic Town 'N Country grocery store Cacciatore Bros. celebrates 125 years as a foodie paradise." Travel "Around Town" with Good Morning Tampa Bay, ABC Action News, WFTS Tampa Bay, February 26, 2021.

Oldest Electric Company
"TECO ENERGY, INC. History." Funding Universe website. http://www.fundinguniverse.com/company-histories/teco-energy-inc-history/

Oldest Theater
Kelley, McKenna. "Made in Tampa: Centro Asturiano." *Tampa Magazine*, November 20, 2019.; Wikipedia contributors, "Centro Asturiano de Tampa," *Wikipedia, The Free Encyclopedia*, https://en.wikipedia.org/w/index.php?title=Centro_Asturiano_de_Tampa&oldid=1058659922 (accessed July 1, 2022).

Oldest Catholic Church
"History." Sacred Heart Catholic Church website. https://sacredheartfla.org/about-us/history/; Wikipedia contributors. "Sacred Heart Catholic Church (Tampa, Florida)." *Wikipedia, The Free Encyclopedia*. https://en.wikipedia.org/w/index.php?title=Sacred_Heart_Catholic_Church_(Tampa,_Florida)&oldid=1072592375 (accessed July 1, 2022).

Oldest Country Club
"About the Club." Tampa Yacht & Country Club website, https://www.tampayacht.com/club; Rajtar, Steve. *A Guide to Historic Tampa Florida*. Charleston, SC: The History Press, 2007.

Oldest Restaurant
"Florida's Oldest Restaurant History." Columbia Restaurant website. https://www.columbiarestaurant.com/The-Columbia-Experience/History; Johnson, Diann. "A Brief History of the Columbia Restaurant in Tampa, FL." Culture Trip, October 3, 2018. https://theculturetrip.com/north-america/usa/florida/articles/a-brief-history-of-the-columbia-restaurant-in-tampa-fl/

Oldest Public Playground
"The History of Playgrounds and the First Playgrounds." AAA State of Play website. https://www.aaastateofplay.com/history-of-playgrounds/; "Kate Veronica Jackson." Friends of the Tampa Riverwalk website. https://thetampariverwalk.com/visit/historical-monument-trail.html/title/kate-veronica-jackson; Kamm, Grayson. "Why do they call it that? Best mayor Tampa never had." 10 Tampa Bay, WTSP, July 26, 2013.

Oldest Golf Course
"History." Rocky Point Golf Course website. https://www.rockypointgolf.net/history; Wikipedia contributors. "Rocky Point Golf Course (Tampa, FL)." *Wikipedia, The Free Encyclopedia*. https://en.wikipedia.org/w/index.php?title=Rocky_Point_Golf_Course_(Tampa,_FL)&oldid=976000600 (accessed July 1, 2022).; Berlinicke, Jeff. "Tampa's Rocky Point Golf Course gives golfers a look at the way it used to be." FloridaGolf.com by Gold Advisor, July 12, 2011. http://www.floridagolf.com/articles/rocky-point-golf-course-tampa-12321.htm

Oldest Train Station
"The History of Tampa Union Station." Tampa Union Station website. http://www.tampaunionstation.com/history/; Rasmussen, Holden. "Tampa Union Station, The station that unified Tampa." Tampa Historical, University of South Florida. https://tampahistorical.org/items/show/165

Oldest Bakery
"About Alessi Bakery." Alessi Bakery website. https://www.alessibakery.com/about/; Kelley, McKenna. "Made in Tampa: Alessi Bakery." *Tampa Magazine*, September 19, 2018. https://tampamagazines.com/alessi-bakery/; Amick, Brian. "Tampa Bay bakery celebrates 108th anniversary." *Bake*, September 28, 2020. https://www.bakemag.com/articles/13870-tampa-bay-bakery-celebrates-108th-anniversary

Oldest High-Rise Building
"Hortense the Beautiful." Tampa Pix website. https://www.tampapix.com/oldcityhall.htm tour0655. "Historic Tampa City Hall." Tampa Bay Foundation for Architecture & Design, June 13, 2012. http://tourtampabayarchitecture.com/page 9-html; Rajtar, Steve. *A Guide to Historic Tampa Florida*. Charleston, SC: The History Press, 2007.

Oldest Bicycle Shop
Mundie, Jessica. "This Tampa bike shop fixes hearts, people too." *Tampa Bay Times*, December 31, 2005.; Dawson, Anastasia. "Bike man Joe Haskins, who kept his struggling neighbors on the road, dead at 79." *Tampa Bay Times*, March 24, 2021.; Lewis, Bobby. "Community shows support after death of iconic Tampa Heights bike shop owner." 10 Tampa Bay, WTSP, March 25, 2021.

Oldest Radio Station
Miller, Jeff. "History of WDAE, Tampa." Some Tampa-St. Petersberg Radio History website. https://jeff560.tripod.com/wdae.html; "WDAE AM & FM – A History." Radio Years website. http://www.radioyears.com/other/details.cfm?id=431

Oldest Streetcar
"Tampa Streetcar Fest 2004–Birney #163–Page 9." Tampa Pix. https://www.tampapix.com/fest09.htm; Staff Writer. "Looking Back: The Ybor City Streetcar gets a new life (Dec. 27, 1991)." *Tampa Bay Times*, July 20, 2017.; "Streetcar Vehicles." TECO Line Streetcar System. http://www.tecolinestreetcar.org/assets/documents/StreetcarVehicles.pdf; Kite-Powell, Rodney. "Tampa's Streetcar History." Tampa Bay History Center. http://tampabayhistorycenter.blogspot.com/2014/02/tampas-streetcar-history.html

Oldest Facility Specifically Designed as Senior Housing
Wikipedia contributors. "Old People's Home (Tampa, Florida)." *Wikipedia, The Free Encyclopedia*. https://en.wikipedia.org/w/index.php?title=Old_People%27s_Home_(Tampa,_Florida)&oldid=1015027826 (accessed July 1, 2022).; "Florida Historical Markers Programs – Marker: Hillsborough." Florida Department of State. http://apps.flheritage.com/markers/markers.cfm?county=hillsborough#:~:text=Description%3A%20Opened%20in%201924%2C%20The,only%20as%20Trustees%20or%20Advisors

Oldest Racetrack
Wikipedia contributors. "Tampa Bay Downs." *Wikipedia, The Free Encyclopedia*. https://en.wikipedia.org/w/index.php?title=Tampa_Bay_Downs&oldid=1090927936 (accessed July 1, 2022).; "Tampa Bay Downs." America's Best Racing website. https://www.americasbestracing.net/tracks/tampa-bay-downs; "History." Tampa Bay Downs website. https://www.tampabaydowns.com/visitor-info/visitors-information/about-tampa-bay-downs/history-of-tampa-bay-downs

Oldest Hospital
"History of Tampa General Hospital." Tampa General Hospital website. https://www.tgh.org/about-tgh/tgh-history

Oldest Airfield
"The History of Tampa International Airport." Tampa International Airport website. http://www.tampaairport.com/history/; "Drew Field." Tampa Pix website. https://www.tampapix.com/drewfield.htm; Wikipedia contributors. "Tampa International Airport." *Wikipedia, The Free Encyclopedia*. https://en.wikipedia.org/w/index.php?title=Tampa_International_Airport&oldid=1095749708 (accessed July 1, 2022).

Oldest Preserved Rooming House
"Who We Are?" Bing Rooming House Museum website. http://www.plantcitybinghouse.com/about-2/; "Bing Rooming House African American Museum." Visit Florida website. https://www.visitflorida.com/listing/bing-rooming-house-african-american-museum/15068/

Oldest Family-Owned Jewelers
"Our Story." Hayman Jewelry Co. website. https://haymanjewelry.com/about-hayman-jewelry-co/

Oldest Nudist and Naturist Resort
Lake Como Nudist and Naturalist Resort website. https://www.lakecomonaturally.com/forms/lakecomohistory.pdf
Harnisch, Lukas. "Naked And Unafraid: The Nudist Capital Of The World." Wonderlust. https://wonderlusttravel.com/pasco-county-florida-the-nudist-capital-of-the-world/; Pittman, Craig. "The State You're In." University Press of Florida, Gainesville, FL, 2022.

Oldest Bar
Guzzo, Paul. "The Hub, downtown Tampa's beloved dive bar, turns 70 – maybe." *Tampa Bay Times*. August 27, 2019.

Oldest Ice Cream Parlor
"Generations enjoy Bo's Ice Cream since 1954." Fox 13 Tampa Bay, June 30, 2017.; Harlan, Andrew. "Tampa Treasures: Bo's Ice Cream." That's So Tampa, July 18, 2019. https://thatssotampa.com/tampa-treasures-bos-ice-cream/; Brink, Graham. "How sweet it is." *Tampa Bay Times*, August 28, 2005. https://www.tampabay.com/archive/2004/10/29/how-sweet-it-is/; "Bo's Ice Cream Shop." Tampa Pix website. https://www.tampapix.com/bos.htm

Oldest Family-Owned Premium Cigar Factory
"Our Family." J.C. Newman website. https://www.jcnewman.com/our-family/; Savona, David. "Last Men Standing." Cigar Aficionado, December 2009.; Simonson, Jennifer. "The Last Cigar Factory in Tampa." *Smithsonian Magazine*, January 7, 2020.; Rajtar, Steve. *A Guide to Historic Tampa Florida*. Charleston, SC: The History Press, 2007.

Oldest Bowling Alley
Guzzo, Paul. "Tampa's Pin Chasers celebrates its 60th anniversary." *Tampa Bay Times*,

March 13, 2019.; "60th Anniversary." Pin Chasers website. https://pinchasers.net/sixtieth-anny/it-all-started-with-bill-and-the-hot-florida-sun/

Oldest Theme Park
McMorrow-Hernandez, Joshua. *Busch Gardens Tampa Bay*. Arcadia Publishing, March 13, 2017.; "Busch Gardens Africa." Tampa Pix website. https://www.tampapix.com/buschgardens10.htm

Oldest State Historical Marker
"History." Henry B. Plant Museum website. https://www.plantmuseum.com/; "Tampa Bay Hotel, 1891: Other Nearby Markers, Tampa Bay Hotel." The Historical Marker Database. https://www.hmdb.org/m.asp?m=20063

Oldest Enclosed Shopping Center
Wikipedia contributors. "WestShore Plaza." *Wikipedia, The Free Encyclopedia*. https://en.wikipedia.org/w/index.php?title=WestShore_Plaza&oldid=1039548735 (accessed July 1, 2022).; "West Shore Plaza Shopping City." Mall Hall of Fame website. http://mall-hall-of-fame.blogspot.com/2007/07/colonial-plaza-colonial-drive-and-bumby.html

Oldest Skyscraper
Griffin, Justine. "Park Tower building in downtown Tampa to be upgraded." *Tampa Bay Times*, June 6, 2017.; Wikipedia contributors. "Park Tower (Tampa)." *Wikipedia, The Free Encyclopedia*. https://en.wikipedia.org/w/index.php?title=Park_Tower_(Tampa)&oldid=1043682574 (accessed July 1, 2022).

Oldest Thai Buddhist Temple
"About Wat Tampa." Wat Tampa website. https://wattampainenglish.com/wat-tampa/about-wat-tampa.html; Wikipedia contributors. "Wat Mongkolratanaram (Tampa, Florida)." *Wikipedia, The Free Encyclopedia*. https://en.wikipedia.org/w/index.php?title=Wat_Mongkolratanaram_(Tampa,_Florida)&oldid=1086927273 (accessed July 1, 2022).; "Thai Temple Tampa." *The Florida Guidebook*, November 29, 2021. https://www.florida-guidebook.com/thai-temple-tampa/

Oldest Hindu Temple
"About Us History of Hindu Temple of Florida." Hindu Temple of Florida website. https://htfl.org/about-us/; Tcgarner. "Hindu Temple of Florida." Atlas Obscura website. https://www.atlasobscura.com/places/hindu-temple-of-florida; Johnson, Diann. "A Brief History of the Hindu Temple of Florida." Culture Trip, March 21, 2018. https://theculturetrip.com/north-america/usa/florida/articles/a-brief-history-of-the-hindu-temple-of-florida/; Scott, Larissa. "Hindu Temple of Florida celebrates 25 years in Carrollwood." ABC Action News, WFTS Tampa Bay, June 25, 2021.

Oldest Comic Book Shop
Green Shift Comics, Facebook website. https://www.facebook.com/Green-Shift-Comics-481841575187775/

Oldest All-Female Gasparilla Pirate Krewe
Kaserman, James and Sarah Kaserman. *Florida Pirates: From the Southern Gulf Coast to the Keys and Beyond*. Charleston, SC: The History Press 2011.; "About Us." Ye Loyal Krewe of Grace O'Malley website. https://www.kreweofgraceomalley.com/about-us

Oldest Skatepark
Skatepark of Tampa, Youtube Videos. https://www.youtube.com/c/SPoTTampa/videos; Wikipedia contributors. "Skatepark of Tampa." *Wikipedia, The Free Encyclopedia*. https://en.wikipedia.org/w/index.php?title=Skatepark_of_Tampa&oldid=1039501090 (accessed July 1, 2022).

Oldest Tattoo Parlor
Blue Devil Tattoo website. https://www.bluedeviltattoo.com

Oldest Hillsborough County Dog Parks
Greenberg, Alissa. "How Dog Parks Took Over the Urban Landscape." *Smithsonian Magazine*, January 7, 2020.

Oldest Alligator Attraction
"History." Croc Encounters website. https://www.crocencounters.com/history.html

Oldest Gold Star Family Memorial Monument
Woody Williams Foundation website. https://woodywilliams.org/; Lewis, Bobby. "Middle school's Gold Star monument serves as a lesson in sacrifice." 10 Tampa Bay, WTSP, October 28, 2019.

Oldest Preserved Open-Water Wooden Canoe
Tomalin, Terry, and the *St. Petersburg Times*. "40-foot canoe in St. Petersburg 'very important historical find.'" *Orlando Sentinel*, May 27, 2008.; Weedon Island Preserve Website. http://www.weedonislandpreserve.org/prehistoric-canoe.htm

Oldest Preserved Two-Story Family Home
"McMullen-Coachman Log Cabin: A Brief Introduction." https://digitalcommons.usf.edu/cgi/viewcontent.cgi?filename=6&article=4026&context=fac_publications&type=additional

Oldest Public Library
"History of the Library." City of Dunedin website. www.dunedingov.com/city-departments/library/about/history-of-the-library

Oldest Hotel
Wikipedia contributors. "Belleview-Biltmore Hotel." *Wikipedia, The Free Encyclopedia*. https://en.wikipedia.org/w/index.php?title=Belleview-Biltmore_Hotel&oldid=1085185299 (accessed July 1,

2022).; "Belleview Inn." Historic Hotels of America website. https://www.historichotels.org/us/hotels-resorts/belleview-inn/history.php; "Belleview Inn Story." Belleview Inn website. https://www.thebelleviewinn.com/the-belleview-story/the-history/the-historic-hotel/

Oldest Incorporated Beach Community in Pinellas County
United States Department of the Interior National Park Service, National Register of Historic Places Continuation Sheet for the Pass-a-Grille Historic District, September, 1989.

Oldest Family-Owned Shoe Repair Shop
Rosenfield, Jeff. "Lasting legacy: For three generations the Faklis family's shoe store has served as a cornerstone of downtown Tarpon Springs." *Suncoast News*, September 22, 2020.; Staff Writer. "Faklis, Tarapani families celebrate 100 years in department store business in Tarpon Springs." *Tampa Bay Times*, December 1, 2012.

Oldest Open Air Post Office
"History Breezes Through the Open Air Post Office." *Green Bench Monthly*, August 8, 2018.

Oldest Museum
Hartzell, Scott Taylor. "A 'doer' extraordinaire makes history in 1920." *Tampa Bay Times*, August 25, 1999.; "About St. Petersburg Museum of History." St. Petersburg Museum of History website. http://www.stpetemuseumofhistory.org/about/; Wolf, Colin. "St. Pete Museum of History announces plans for a new 8,000-square-foot expansion," Creative Loafing, July 30, 2019. https://www.cltampa.com/news/st-pete-museum-of-history-announces-plans-for-a-new-8000squarefoot-expansion-12182935

Oldest Health Spa
"Safety Harbor Resort & Spa." Tennis Resorts Online website. https://www.tennisresortsonline.com/trofiles/safety-harbor-resort-and-spa.cfm; "Safety Harbor Resort and Spa." Florida Stories Walking Tours website. https://floridastories.oncell.com/en/safety-harbor-resort-and-spa-189078.html; "Safety Harbor Resort & Spa." Historic Hotels of America website. https://www.historichotels.org/us/hotels-resorts/safety-harbor-resort-and-spa/history.php; Ramos, Jillian. "Safety Harbor Resort and Spa celebrates 95 years." ABC Action News, WFTS Tampa Bay, August 20, 2021. https://www.abcactionnews.com/news/region-pinellas/safety-harbor-resort-and-spa-celebrates-95-years

Oldest Roadside Attraction
"Sunken Gardens." City of St. Petersburg website. https://www.stpete.org/visitors/sunken_gardens.php; Ginsberg, Joshua. *Secret Tampa Bay: A Guide to the Weird, Wonderful and Obscure*. St. Louis: Reedy Press, 2021.

Oldest Architecture Firm
"History." Harvard Jolly Architecture website. https://www.harvardjolly.com//history; Erickson, Chris. "Tampa Bay's oldest architecture firm remains the area's largest." *Tampa Bay Business Journal*, July 19, 2016.

Oldest Diner
"About." The Chattaway website. https://thechattaway.com/about/; Basse, Craig. "Co-owner of Chattaway Drive-In dies." *Tampa Bay Times*, September 2, 2005.; Barack, Lauren. "Landmark Chattaway restaurant up for sale." *Tampa Bay Times*, July 12, 1995.

Oldest Video Arcade
"Treasure Island Fun Center." Visit St. Pete Clearwater website. https://www.visitstpeteclearwater.com/profile/treasure-island-fun-center/140009

Oldest Independent Weekly Newspaper
"About the Gabber." *Gabber* website. https://thegabber.com/about-the-gabber/

Oldest Artist Retreat
Baker, Abby. "Blueberry Patch Returns After Two-Year Hiatus." *The Gabber*, June 16, 2021.; Pendygraft, John. "In this Blueberry Patch, free spirits thrive." *Tampa Bay Times*, January 4, 2015.; Meacham, Andrew. "Gulfport's Blueberry Patch founder Dallas Bohrer dies at 81." *Tampa Bay Times*, July 11, 2014.

Oldest Microbrewery
DeNote, Mark. *Tampa Bay Beer, A Heady History*, American Palate (a division of History Press). Charleston, SC, 2015.; "Who is Dunedin Brewery?" Dunedin Brewery website. https://dunedinbrewery.com/info

Oldest Paranormal Investigators
SPIRITS of St. Petersburg website. http://www.spiritsofstpete.com

Oldest Escape Room
Tampa Bay Escape Room website. https://tampabayescaperoom.com; "The History of Escape Rooms (2021)." The Escape Game blog, March 31, 2021. https://theescapegame.com/blog/the-history-of-escape rooms/#:~:text=Early%20%E2%80%9CEscape%20The%20Room%E2%80%9D%20Games,and%2Dclick%20style%20of%20gameplay

Oldest Preserved Plantation House
Hardy, Michael. "The Sad Truth About Florida's Gamble Mansion & Plantation Before and During The Civil War." May 3, 2021. https://thumbwind.com/2021/05/03/gamble-plantation/; Gross, Bonnie. "Gamble Mansion: Civil War history near Sarasota." FloridaRambler.com, May 8, 2021. https://www.floridarambler.com/historic-florida-getaways/gamble-mansion-florida-civil-war/

Oldest Preserved County Courthouse
"A Courthouse for the New County," Manatee Village Website, https://express.adobe.com/page/2jQUdZM52Am2V

Oldest Commercial Ice House
Metro / Manatee Ice Co. website. https://www.metroicecompany.com/

Oldest Sarasota Celebrity Estate
"Bertha Honore Palmer – 1849 – 1918." Buy Sarasota website. https://www.buysarasota.com/bertha-honore-palmer.php; "Mrs. Bertha Palmer's Vision." Sarasota County History Center. http://www.sarasotahistoryalive.com/history/people/mrs.-bertha-palmer-s-vision/; Smith, Jessi. "Bertha Palmer: The Woman Who Tamed Wild Sarasota." Visit Sarasota website, December 31, 2020. https://www.visitsarasota.com/article/bertha-palmer-woman-who-tamed-wild-sarasota#:~:text=When%20the%20millionaire%20matron%20of,that%20most%20assumed%20was%20uninhabitable; LaHurd, Jeff. *Hidden History of Sarasota*. Charleston, SC: The History Press 2009.

Oldest Family-Owned Department Store Chain
"A Century of History." Bealls website. https://www.beallsflorida.com/online/about-us; Gordon, Mark. "Beall's 100-year anniversary." *Business Observer*, July 3, 2015.

Oldest Minor League Baseball Stadium
"LECOM Park." MLB website. https://www.mlb.com/pirates/spring-training/ballpark; "Why Do the Pittsburgh Pirates Love McKechnie Field?" Florida Dreams Realty of Anna Maria Island blog. https://www.florida-dreams.com/why-do-the-pittsburgh-pirates-love-mckechnie-field/#:~:text=LECOM%20Park%20originally%20opened%20in,capacity%20to%208%2C500%20in%202013.; Wikipedia contributors. "LECOM Park." *Wikipedia, The Free Encyclopedia*. https://en.wikipedia.org/w/index.php?title=LECOM_Park&oldid=1093045079 (accessed July 1, 2022).

Oldest Youth Circus
"Our History." The Circus Arts Conservatory website. https://circusarts.org/programs/history/; Mancini, Mary Ellen. "The Oldest Youth Circus In America Lives In Sarasota." Visit Sarasota County website. https://www.visitsarasota.com/article/oldest-youth-circus-america-lives-sarasota

Oldest Antique Car Museum
"History." Sarasota Classic Car Museum website. https://www.sarasotacarmuseum.org/history/; "Sarasota Classic Car Museum." Must Do Visitor Guides. https://www.mustdo.com/fl/sarasota-gulf-islands-venice-bradenton/attractions/sarasota-classic-car-museum/

Oldest Tiki Bar
Buchanan, Dave. "From Donn Beach to Polynesian Pop: The History of Tiki Cocktail Culture." KegWorks blog, June 30, 2021. https://content.kegworks.com/blog/history-of-tiki-cocktail-culture#:~:text=Tiki%20goes%20mainstream%20in%20post,up%20all%20over%20the%20country; Geurts, Jimmy. "Sarasota's Bahi Hut remains a classic piece of tiki bar history." Herald-Tribune, July 31, 2019.

Oldest Opera Company
"About Sarasota Opera." Sarasota Opera website. https://www.sarasotaopera.org/about-sarasota-opera-house

Oldest Surf Shop
Shaw, Matthew B. "Florida's Oldest Surf Shop Gets New Life." *Surfer*, February 18, 2019. https://www.surfer.com/features/floridas-oldest-surf-shop-gets-new-life/

Oldest Tennis Academy
"About IMG Academy." IMG Academy website. https://www.imgacademy.com/; Wikipedia contributors, "IMG Academy," *Wikipedia, The Free Encyclopedia*. https://en.wikipedia.org/w/index.php?title=IMG_Academy&oldid=1095080306 (accessed July 1, 2022).

Oldest Bird Sanctuary and Wildlife Rehab Facility
"History & More." Save Our Seabirds website. https://www.saveourseabirds.org/our-impact; Valine, Kevin and Patty Allen-Jones. "Dale 'Pelican Man' Shields dies; founded bird shelter." Herald-Tribune, January 3, 2003.

INDEX